The Boy from Hilltop

by

Thomas L. Trigg

DORRANCE PUBLISHING CO
EST. 1920
PITTSBURGH, PENNSYLVANIA 15238

Dorrance Publishing Co
585 Alpha Drive
Pittsburgh, PA 15238
Visit our website at www.dorrancebookstore.com

ISBN: 979-8-88925-295-5
eISBN: 979-8-88925-795-0

April 30ᵗʰ, 1947, Tacoma, Washington, I was born at St. Joseph's hospital around 9 A.M. Not sure if it was a nice day but probably didn't matter because I couldn't see much anyway. Tacoma, Washington in 1947 was a typical post WW2 town with lots of returning GI's looking for a place to work and live. Tacoma, being a blue-collar town, was a great place to begin or restart a life. Lots of shipyard work, papermills, small factories, and hard-working able bodied men and women from pioneer stock. That little slice of Tacoma I was brought into was called Hilltop. The part of Hilltop we lived in was K Street, later to be called Martin Luther King Way. Now K Street, as it was called when I was a kid, bordered Little Italy. My grandparents who immigrated from Southern Italy and Sicily settled on Ainsworth Avenue, right smack dab in the heart of little Italy. Now there were some Swedes and Germans mixed in there but mostly Italians. Years later, when I went to Coscenza, Italy to visit my grandmother's village, the local church looked exactly like St. Rita's church just down the block from Nana's house. All the Italian Catholics in Little Italy went to St. Rita's. It was where you got your first communion, first confession, confirmed, married, and counselled by the parish priest, Father Baffaro. Didn't matter if he didn't know about Freud's repression and suppression theories. There was sin and forgiveness. That's all you needed to know, and by God you needed to be thankful for the good things in life because depression was an option, not a condition. Masturbation was a mortal sin, and if you died without going to confession, you were going to hell forever. No purgatory for you. If you missed mass, that was another mortal sin. It was easy to just give up and say to hell with it. No wonder the mafia could flip from family first to murder incorporated. Didn't matter, the extremes were easy to accommodate. Down at the other end of the block was Manza's grocery, a little mom and pop grocery where you bought your milk, bread, candy, and maybe some meat. My grandparents didn't have a refrigerator in Little Italy, just a little cold box and maybe an ice box where the ice man delivered a block of ice. The Italians had their own little gardens, and in Nana and Papa's case, that garden supplied all their vegetables for the entire year. Papa made his own wine in the cellar. They knew how to can foods, how to graft fruit trees, and all within a small city lot. As I recall, everyone seemed to get along pretty well. My grandfather, Papa, was from a small Sicilian village called San Cipirello, Sicily, right next door to Corleone. I visited there and was surprised by the impression that nothing had changed in a hundred years. A street was named after my grandfather's family name, the street of Tropiano. In Hilltop, the Swedes, Germans, and Italians had respect for each other but remained separate into their own little neighborhood. K Street, where I was living at age four, was a little different. There were lots of lower income people living as tenants in rental apartments and some mentally ill people. At night the bums would sometimes sleep under the apple tree in our front yard. Susie Q, the neighbor lady, would wander over to our house and bother us when she was drunk. Our Great Dane dog was a good deterrent for the more aggressive types. Our Great Dane, Bernie, would jump over the six-foot fence, and we would get a call to come and get him. We had to take the city bus because there wasn't room in our car for him. My dad was in Alaska working, so it was up to my mom to get him. I just remember the bus driver wasn't happy about having a Great Dane on the bus. One day Mr. Johnson, who owned Johnson Candy Company across the street, came to my mom's rescue because a bum decided to sleep on our porch and my mom didn't want to deal with him, so Mr. Johnson made the bum leave. My little friend, Kenny Love and I, would hang out under the corner apple tree where the drunks would congregate at night and drink their little bottles of whiskey. One time I fell out of the tree and cut my foot on the broken whiskey bottles. I have no idea why I wasn't wearing my shoes. There was no dress code for a four-year-old. It wasn't a big deal, but Kenny's father was a different matter. Kenny's dad had returned from Korea and had been shot, and the bullet just grazed his head. His helmet had a bullet hole in the helmet liner. When he drank, he was a scary guy. He used to grab me and pretend to cut my ear off with his little knife. Kenny and I would play with the older kids, aka the K street gangs, and dodge bb gun pellets in the alley behind our house. There were lots of veterans around, which I later discovered when going to work with my dad at American Lake VA hospital. Now my dad worked at Tacoma General Hospital just down a few blocks from where we lived at 10th and K Street. Johnson's Candy Company was right across the street and is still there seventy years later. There was the Federal bakery, where my Aunt Bev worked, Arden's Malt Shop, where my mom worked part-time, and the Chinese dime store. Next door was the shoe store where you could x-ray your feet to see how the shoe fit. I think that was outlawed due to radiation exposure. Speaking of X-ray. My dad was the X-ray tech at Tacoma General Hospital. I think at that time X-ray technology was coming into its own. A Dr. Regis was head of X-ray, and I know that he suffered from lung cancer probably due to exposure to radiation. I recall watching my dad work with patients, and they didn't have all the precautions that later day labs had. If the call was late at night, there may not be anyone to hold a patient on the table. The broken hips were always painful and difficult to get to move a certain way or hold still for the X-ray. So my dad worked at almost every Tacoma hospital in X-ray either as an employee or on call. I would get to go with him on some calls, and it could be unpleasant. No one wore seat belts or helmets in those days. A minor accident by today's standards could be life ending. Broken hips were often fatal. Hunting season was a busy time. At the county hospital, you would see it all. Anyway it got more interesting when my dad went to work at American Lake VA hospital. That was where you got to see the results of war and the long-term impact for those who survived war. My mom worked at the canteen where the patients would hang out when they were not in their ward. Some were allowed to wander around the grounds unsupervised depending on their status. Some were considered mentally unstable and confined to their rooms. I remember watching patients sitting at a table with a blank stare or the thousand- yard stare while listening to Patsy Cline sing one of her tunes on the juke box. Later I learned that patients would sometimes rotate between the VA hospital and Western State Hospital, the infamous psychiatric facility that would later play a sad chapter in my life.

After a year in the Army, my parents moved to Los Angeles because my dad was transferred to the Long Beach VA Hospital. After a few years there, they moved to the Menlo Park VA Hospital next to Stanford. At that time, during the 1970's, the Vietnam War was drawing down and returning GI's were more often coming in to the hospital for methadone treatment. The VA was cutting costs and would not staff the hospital for the influx of new patients. At night, when patients showed up for admittance, there was a shortage of security staff to protect the staff. Many nights my dad would have to call for extra security because of violent patients demanding drugs. More often than not the security guards would disappear when there was a violent patient. The hospital was also being mismanaged due to lack of funding. Mice were running through the halls and offices. One night a mouse crawled up my dad's pant leg. My dad made a formal complaint to the congressman representing the district. All that happened was they transferred my dad to a different job and promoted around him so he would get the message. This was just the beginning of the problems with lack of funding. The Madigan Army Hospital by Fort Lewis, now Joint Base Lewis- McChord, was ranked as the worst medical facility during this same period for high death rate and incompetent care. The government wanted service men and women to serve their country, but when they returned from active service, didn't want to serve them. It was too easy to cut costs and ignore service members needs once the wars were over. My dad always told me that if I were to join the marines, be sure to be service connected for psychiatric. I didn't understand at that time what he meant. After learning more about what the marines went through in World War II and seeing the after effects at the VA hospital, I figured it out. Not all of us are cut out for the brutality of war and its after effects. The psychological damage (PTSD) can be permanent.

My dad was the product of a World War I soldier from Montana and a London born nurse. My paternal grandfather and grandmother met in a London hospital where my grandfather was being treated for influenza, or the Spanish flu, and shell shock, which ravaged soldiers and half the world. After the war ended in 1918, they moved to Everett Washington where they resided until my father was born. My grandfather, the Everett telegraph operator, disappeared, never to be heard from again. Many years later I researched his disappearance only to discover that many people during that era disappeared, never to be heard from and their body never found. My father was about six-months-old when his father disappeared. My grandmother, Eva, was never sure what happened and believed that he had simply deserted her and their newborn son. That story never bore out because Willie, as he was known, was very close to his mother and he never contacted her after his disappearance. Never the less, my grandmother did harbor resentment towards my father, maybe because he looked a lot like his father, at least in the pictures I saw. Eventually my grandmother met a man who would become my step-grandfather. Ralph Miller was the son of Winfield Miller, a civil war veteran, who moved to Joyce Washington in 1884. Many civil war soldiers, especially from the confederacy, moved as far away as they could to start over. There was a land give away, started by President Lincoln in 1862. The Homestead act encouraged people to move out west. Initially the Homestead Act gave 160 acres to those that chose to take advantage of it. My grandfather married Eva, and they proceeded to log the land and clear the acres for their Joyce farm. There is a road named after Winfield Miller in Joyce, and as I am told, the Millers were some of the first to log the old growth forests in that area. During World War I, the Spruce Corps set up camp to harvest Spruce for the first airplanes. My grandfather ran a logging camp and my father was expected to work on the farm and help clear land. According to my father, he was treated poorly by his mother who seemed to resent his presence. She would take any gifts he received and sell them to the Indians, and in exchange, give him used items. My grandmother would incite her husband, Ralph, to beat my father, and eventually my father ran away. My dad never blamed his step-father because his mother goaded him into punishing my dad. Alcohol had something to do with it also. After several run ins with the juvenile probation officers in Port Angeles, my father was placed in a foster home. It just so happened that the Juvenile probation officer appointed in that area took a liking to my father and brought him into his home and helped raise him. My father was a pretty bright kid by all accounts, and after working in a local hospital in Tacoma, a doctor wanted to pay for my father's education and medical school. My dad was pretty affable and could talk to anyone. Everyone seemed to like him, and finding work was not a problem. The ironic thing about my grandmother was that she was named mother of the year in 1972 because she raised so much money for cystic fibrosis research and donated to Children's Hospital in Seattle. Governor Dan Evans presented her with a plaque, and it was a big deal. If only the public knew the true story about how she treated my father. My grandmother did have two children with Ralph and both were Valedictorian and Salutatorian at the University of Washington. My Uncle Spud was a Colonel in the Marines, and my Aunt Audrey was instrumental in writing part of the book, *Jimmy Come Lately*, the history of Clallam County. When Winfield Miller settled in Joyce, Washington, he became the local postmaster. He married an Indian Princess, and as I understand the history, she came from Vancouver Island. Eventually my grandmother Eva and my dad reconciled, sort of. However, there never was much love from her. Everything was about making money for her charity work. My uncle's son had cystic fibrosis, and that fueled her mission in life to raise money for research into the cure for that deadly disease. Christmas gifts were thoroughly scanned for pests because everything that Eva gave was used, and who knew where she would find her stuff. Often her trips to Tacoma were by way of the landfill, and if she could scrounge scraps that could be resold, she would fill her pick-up truck. I remember seeing her painting old shoes and selling them to the Indians. Often old clothes from the dump would be rechristened as good enough to be sold as used. While at the farm in Joyce, she took me for a haircut. The lady put a bowl on my head and cut my hair, and even at the age of six or seven, I knew that wasn't a good look. In fact Moe from The Three Stooges must have seen her for his haircut. In retrospect my grandmother and step-grandfather were pioneers and survivors of tough conditions. They had no sympathy for whining or as she used to say, "Quit your kicking." Talk about contrasts in living. Going from Hill Top in Tacoma to Joyce, Washington was a definite contrast. At my grandparents farm, you could see the top of the Olympic Mountains from their farm and there was nothing in between, just old growth forest. It was true wilderness.

Hilltop was an interesting place to live in the prewar and post WWII years. K Street, later named MLK Way, was a marketplace where you could shop for appliances, go to a movie, the bakery, drug store, or little shops that offered personal items. After the war, returning GI's were happy to be able to buy a home if one could be found. Salishan was a government housing project set up for war workers in 1942. The housing boom would start to expand into outlying areas, like Fircrest and University Place. Life in Hilltop was relatively safe during the 1950's. People walked, even at night. There were sidewalks and street lights. Not everyone could afford a car, and lots of people took the bus, especially in the city. My Italian grandparents never had a car. They walked to church or the corner grocery store. If they needed to go down town, they took the bus. It was later, in the 1960's, that changed. As the returning GI's and newer generation started to look for places to live, they abandoned the Hilltop. It was then that the culture changed. Within a few years, it was no longer safe to walk through the neighborhood at night and more and more during the daytime hours. Homes were burglarized more frequently, and in my Nana's case, they broke in during the daytime while she was working in the yard. If she went to wait for a bus, there was risk of being mugged and was mugged several times. She never called the police and too proud to give in. The culture had changed from being little Italy to a ghetto. It was only a few years later gun fights broke out between rival drug gangs. There was even a national news story about a gunfight in 1989 between Crips gang members and special forces soldiers in Hilltop. It got worse. A mini war broke out with gun fights, and the media compared it to Watts in LA. People going down town drove around Hilltop rather than through it. Police installed surveillance cameras in intersections to monitor gang drug activity. Long gone were the quaint little homes with gardens. Life in Hilltop was like a prison. If you wanted to drive through Hilltop, the gangs thought you were looking for drugs and would follow your vehicle. Property values dropped, and if you could afford to leave, you did. The damage was done. Hilltop was now a place just like Watts, a place to avoid.

Tacoma was a racist town by today's definition. If there was a group of people that were discriminated against because of their ethnicity, it was the Chinese. In the late 1800's, around 200 Chinese immigrants were rounded up and escorted out of town during a rainstorm in late November 1885. Then the local white folk burned down their businesses and homes. The white townspeople didn't like the idea of Chinese immigrants taking unskilled jobs. The reason the Chinese were there in the first place was because they were brought in to build the railroad and other menial jobs too hard for regular workers. The City of Tacoma built a Chinese Reconciliation Park to commemorate the expulsion of the Chinese in 1885. The park is located near where the Chinese village was burned.

We all learned about the Japanese who were rounded up and interred in prisoner of war camps. The Italians, too, were classified as enemy aliens, along with Germans. If caught in restricted areas, like docks and airbases, they could be imprisoned. From the late 1880's, anti-immigrant societies sprung up. Catholic churches and charities were vandalized and burned. Italians were attacked by mobs. In 1891 in New Orleans, the chief of police was shot dead, and the mayor blamed "Sicilian Gangsters." More than 100 Sicilian Americans were rounded up, and eleven Italians were lynched even after being found not guilty. Over 600,000 Italians were placed on a watch list during WWII and many were rounded up and placed in camps, just like the Japanese. This part of history was covered up because most Italians were embarrassed by this piece of history. It didn't stop there. There was pervasive anti-Italian hostility, even after the war years. Being born from Italian/English parents and taking my father's English name, I was assumed to be of white American heritage. When people told jokes with anti-Italian themes, they didn't suspect I was offended by their ignorance. I witnessed the discrimination when people would be condescending toward my grandfather, Papa, because he spoke with broken English, and when my uncle, a war hero, was overlooked as a potential leader of the local white dominated clubs. They wanted him to cook for them but not lead them. In the Tacoma police department where my uncle worked the hierarchy were white. Both my Italian uncles enlisted in the Army. My Uncle Jack was airborne and fought in the Philippines. He returned home after the war suffering from malaria. Eventually he became a Tacoma motorcycle cop. I know he was a good cop and reputed to be a very tough dude who had your back in a tough town like Tacoma was. Downtown Tacoma on Pacific Avenue was the main thoroughfare where Sears, Penny's, The Bon, and Schoenfeld's Furniture Store were located. Woolworths had a great lunch counter restaurant that was packed most days. The South side of Pacific Avenue was a little seedier. The circus/circus arcade, tattoo shop, Greyhound bus station, and X-rated movie houses dominated the block. I am sure there were other activities that attracted the GI's from Fort Lewis and the reason there was a patty wagon stationed outside the circus, circus arcade. When the Tacoma Mall was built in the 1960's, the main street businesses moved to the mall leaving downtown Tacoma a ghost town after 5:00 P.M. One day my uncle had to climb to the top of 11th Street bridge in Tacoma to talk down a suicidal individual. He discovered that the man was an escapee from Western State Hospital and he claimed that they beat him with soap tied inside of a sock. My uncle was on patrol duty when a drunk driver broadsided him on his police motorcycle. He was hit so hard, he went over the telephone lines on Pacific Avenue. They pronounced him dead until he was revived after several minutes. Every major bone in his body was broken, and he was an inpatient at St. Joseph's hospital in Tacoma for nine months. I remember visiting him at home, and his legs were black up to his knees several years after the accident. The doctor wanted to amputate his legs, but he refused. He would not take pain medication and managed to walk with a cane. There was no pension in those days. Eventually he started an Italian import food company, which sustained the family for several years. He was offered the job of deputy coroner. He was selected for the job because of his experience in combat during the war and having been a motorcycle cop. Being a coroner is not a job that just anyone can handle. I recall his telling me about having to go to the bottom of the Narrows Bridge and recover a suicide victim. Often the suicides were kept confidential to avoid copycat suicide attempts. When a serial killer in Tacoma was on the loose, they kept secret that the perpetrator cut off the breasts of his victims because they needed to know if someone was making a fake confession. I was amazed that he could come home from work and have a semblance of a normal life after seeing the human tragedy that was part of his job. He once told me that because of his near-death experience, he described seeing the bright light and leaving his body. He described being drawn toward this warm bright light and didn't want to return. He felt his wife and three children needed him, so he came back. He said he felt confident that there was an afterlife, and when comforting grieving families after the loss of a loved one, he could honestly speak with and comfort them about their loss. My other uncle, John, was my hero growing up. He went off to California when he was sixteen. Being a happy go lucky, good-looking Italian, he could get jobs wherever he went. There were stories about him being a good boxer. He eventually became a Los Angeles police detective. Because of his dark Italian swarthy looks, he often impersonated prisoners inside the prison system and later testified against the bad guys in court, which placed him in harm's way when they got out. Later on he owned pizza places where I worked as a sixteen-year-old kid. We worked until two in the morning and then we went out to Denny's for breakfast with the staff. One night or early morning, we were sitting in Denny's and a customer across the restaurant was bullying another diner.

My uncle said, "Why don't you leave him alone and mind your own business." The guy started to get up and sat down when he figured out he was going to get his ass kicked. Tiny, our bartender who wasn't tiny, was built like Hoss on *Bonanza* was sitting with us. Uncle John was good friends with Barbara Sinatra's parents. One day they invited my uncle to visit Frank's compound in Rancho Mirage. Uncle John said Frank was a great guy and treated his guests very well. Uncle John just passed away at age ninety-six after a full life having had race horses, businesses, taught cooking in a women's prison, Los Angeles detective and movie extra. He was always ready to laugh and have a good time. Everyone loved Uncle John because he loved people. I remember one time while working in his pizza place in Fullerton, California, one of the new employees he had arrested as a young kid. Uncle John thought he was a good person and needed a break. The employee told me that Uncle John could have put him in jail but instead talked with him and got him going in the right direction. One day cash was missing, and John's partner accused the new employee of stealing the cash. He denied it because it wasn't missing, just misplaced. The partner several years later embezzled $25,000 from the partnership and used it to open a new restaurant.

Tacoma was and is a blue-collar white dominated town. It is an incestuous place to do business where the good ole boy network resides. In my opinion, cultural differences are what seems to define one group as compared to another. If you change the culture, you change the reality. Two parent families generally provide security, both financial and emotional to growing children. The peer pressure of outside groups/gangs is neutralized to some extent. The role model of a stable father and mother is essential to break the cycle of dependency on social service programs, drugs, guns, and crime as a way of life. We all know friends that have a single parent/mother and those children turned out just fine. Maybe there are exceptions to the norm but again if the cultural value is strong family support, there are uncles, grandparents, to support the children when a parent is absent or missing. I am just guessing, but it seems to me that family is the main factor in cultural differences, not skin color. Black, white, yellow, or brown is just a label without much else to offer. I know there are factors that prevent this ideal scenario where two parents are role models. Some people should not be married or have children. An abusive parent with addiction problems or anger issues isn't better than no parent. It is easy to generalize when looking from a distance. I am just saying there seem to be factors that are noticeable when thinking about the cultural differences. Anyone trying to understand the growing trend of single parent families is accused of being racist or sexist. How is that connected to Hilltop? Because it is obvious there are/were cultural differences from one ethnic group to another and the quality of life regressed dramatically within a short period of time. Anyone that grew up during this period or was aware of what was happening and could see it evolving right around them. You didn't have to live in Hilltop to be a witness. I do believe that there is racism against people just because of their skin color. I know several black ladies that were pulled over by the police for driving while black. One lady drives an older Cadillac and the other a newer BMW. Both were pulled over driving late at night. One lady was arrested because her eyes were dilated. While incarcerated, she was allowed or told to shower. The arresting officer came into the shower area to watch her, and there was nothing she could do.

We moved to University Place, west of Hilltop, when I was about five-years-old. It was a different experience. There were no bums in the front yard sleeping under the apple tree. The suburbs were just starting to develop, and little Italy in Hilltop was now inhabited by grandparents. Instead of a prewar fixer upper, we lived in a new three-bedroom rambler with a small yard. We walked to school where there were twelve grades all in one building. It was an amazing experience to see everyone in one place with wonder about what the older kids were doing and watching both girls and boys interact. There was a sense of mystery about it all. To go into the older grades areas was forbidden, which made it more interesting. What would happen to you if you got caught inside the hallways of the higher grades? No one knew, which made it more exciting. My mom was the ice cream lady and ran the school store. Within a few years, it all changed when the schools were separated by class size and age. The new junior and senior high school were built several miles away from the old school. Missing was the continuity of everyone being together. It was a great place to grow up. We didn't have a cell phone or computer games to keep us occupied. We had to entertain ourselves. We created projects. For example my friend Les across the street had a chemistry set. We made little explosives like pipe bombs that we used to blow up small trees in the woods. We would ride our bicycles with pipe bombs strapped to our handlebars, not thinking what would happen if we crashed. We made gas model airplanes and went down to Titlow Beach and flew the planes by wire until they crashed. We had soap box derby races with homemade carts from found lumber. We made camps in the woods and rode our bicycles on trips to neighboring towns. We went to the local marina and fished off the pier. Sometimes we would hike over the Narrows Bridge or spend the night under the stars. During hydro races, we would make wood hydros and tow them behind our bicycles and look for mud puddles to pull them through. We went hunting with bb guns and bows and arrows. I slept with my baseball glove and lived for recess when we could practice playing ball. Every day was an adventure. We could ride our bikes to the beach and always find something interesting to do there. Sometimes we would be juvenile delinquents and do damage to homes under construction. Nothing terrible by today's standards. We had sports teams for every sport, and I played tennis by myself against the school wall when bored. When we were not doing something fun, my dad always had projects for me to work on. I mowed lawns with a push mower for fifty cents. If I was assigned a chore and didn't complete it, the belt was my punishment. Girls were a mystery but an exciting part of growing up. We would stake out a pretty girl's house and ride by to see if we could catch a glimpse. Being only nine-years-old, we were not considered a threat.

Most times the girls would giggle and run inside. The only excitement we could realize was imagined. There were no Playboy magazines available, just our own drawings, and while crude, they served the purpose. Considering everything life was pretty innocent.

University Place schools had/have an excellent reputation for quality of teaching staff. George R. Curtis, former principal and later superintendent, knew every students' name, at least when the grades were all combined in one building. He had a reputation for only hiring the very best faculty. For that reason, the school became more like a college and less like just another high school. My mom became the school librarian, so for me it was unlikely I could get away with anything without her knowing about it. One time I broke a light in a hallway playing ball indoors, and within ten minutes, I was called in to the principal's office where my mom was standing next to the vice principal. I tended to gravitate towards the trouble makers, which was a problem, but I did have high ideals, so I was conflicted. I was just getting going with becoming part of a group when my dad decided to move again to be closer to work in Seattle. The Beacon Hill VA hospital in Seattle was too long a drive from University Place, and even though my mom had a good job at the high school, we moved east of Kent, Washington. Now Kent at that time was pretty much an old farming community. East of Kent was undeveloped with a few small farms and not much in the way of services. You had to drive five miles to the store. We used to joke that throwing rocks at the old Coca Cola sign was something to do. There wasn't much mystery to the area. We played touch football in the cow pasture and there was the time one of the low life neighbors got a 30-30 rifle for Christmas, which he used to shoot the poor black neighbor's pig. I didn't see much redeeming living in the area, and the schools were definitely below par. There was an air of hopelessness about the place. After a year, or less than two years, we moved to Federal Way, Washington. This was another pit stop on the road to better places to live. Federal Way was basically a truck stop turned into a Boeing bedroom community with a lot of Boeing workers buying houses that were being developed during the housing bubble after the war years. Fortunately my new neighbors were Chuck and Toni Good. They moved from Pennsylvania to be near Boeing where their dad and mom worked. Chuck was a charmer with good looks but a hair trigger temper. He could knock you out with one punch and often did at Grotto's drive in restaurant. I saw that look in his face more than once and knew what was going to happen next. I think it was a trait from his father, who had once been a tough merchant marine.

However, I didn't see him do anything that would justify calling him a bad guy. One time Chuck's dog, a standard poodle, was misbehaving and Chuck had a baseball bat that he was winding up to hit the dog. I knew that look and stopped him before he could take a swing. We had always had animals, and I loved dogs. I couldn't tolerate anyone abusing an animal. Another friend, Gary Morfield, was basically a nice kid. However, his dad, an ex-marine that had served in some of the roughest fighting in the Pacific, was a scary dude. He would sit and watch TV drinking beer and smoking his Tareyton cigarettes. When his mood soured, he was dangerous. Gary and his siblings were abused, and it showed. Gary could be unpredictable, and if he got it in his head to take a swing at you, he would. I would see his dad show up at the grocery store where I boxed groceries, and he had that belligerent look on his face that said just give me an excuse to take your head off. Whenever I was around Gary and his dad was there, I steered clear of his dad. I knew Gary had the shit beat out of him by his dad for getting caught stealing a car. One night Gary and I hitchhiked about ten miles up to Kent to meet up with another bad dude named John James to get some beer. I didn't even like beer, but it seemed like something to do. Once we got there about one in the morning, there wasn't any beer. Since Gary had been in juvenile detention for stealing a car, he didn't want to get caught out after curfew. So we walked back all the way through the Kent Valley, walking through cow pastures. We were in the middle of the Smith Dairy Farm pastures when we figured out that the fog was so thick, we couldn't see where we were going. Sloshing around in mud and cow manure in the middle of winter was one of those experiences I won't forget. When we finally got back to Gary's place, we couldn't go into the house because we would wake up his father. We broke into a neighbors' trailer and slept on the unheated floor until morning light. We both had hypothermia but didn't know what that was. I crawled in my bedroom window and went to bed for ten hours. Chuck Good, my neighbor, and I had a lot of experiences that were memorable. Girls were not a problem for Chuck. He would screw anything he could and he was a charmer. He didn't respect social niceties though, and more than once he crossed the line. One day in high school, an upper classman called me out into the hallway outside the cafeteria. He claimed to be defending a girl that he liked, but she liked me. He wanted to fight and started throwing punches. We were separated by the mass of students that came out to watch. Chuck decided that he would end it by calling the kid a prick and decking him. They hauled the kid to the hospital with a concussion. After school his buddies hauled me by the arms outside where the football coach stopped them and told them if they wanted to work me over, they had to do it off school grounds. Federal Way was definitely different than University Place. There were two car clubs, the Sultans and the Gear Lords. The Gear Lords were from Auburn and the Sultans were from Federal Way. When the two clubs would meet, it was like Westside Story. By the time I was a senior, there were about five or six deaths due to driving while intoxicated. This was a confusing time to be growing up because there were the ideals everyone was supposed to live up to, but that wasn't what was happening with the people I knew. It seemed there was a violent side to life that was just beneath the surface.

During the high school years at Federal Way, I was working most of the time. I worked at Johnny's Food Center boxing groceries and at Rose's Restaurant cutting chickens, washing dishes, and stayed later to buff floors after the restaurant closed. I would ride my Honda S 90 home regardless of weather. Somehow I graduated from high school and I had no plans to go to college. The day I graduated, there was a draft notice in the mail box waiting for me. The Vietnam war had been going on for a few years, and we had heard of some students that had been killed in action. My dad drove me to the enlistment center in Puyallup, Washington to discuss options with the recruiter. After a few tests, the recruiter offered me a four-year enlistment with the Army Security Agency. He told me a top-secret security clearance was required, and based on my test scores and lack of criminal history, I should qualify.

Off I go to Fort Ord, California. I flew in a 707 aircraft to San Francisco. We, other new recruits, walked around downtown San Francisco in a seedy part of town and arrived at Ford Ord after a bus trip from San Francisco in the middle of the night. We were told to form up and shut up. From that moment on, we were the property of the United States Army. Basic training was the first-time many soldiers had ever been away from home. It was a culture shock to have someone yelling in your face, fatigues that smelled of moth balls, eating in less than five minutes, and not knowing what was going to happen next. We figured they had been doing this for a 100 years, so maybe they knew what they were doing. The difference was and we understood that a lot of these drill instructors had been in Vietnam and knew what we were going to experience. Their job was to train us for combat, and there was no joking about it. Some of these recruits were going to die in the jungles of Vietnam. There wasn't anything you could do about it. Fort Ord was probably as good a place to have basic training as anyplace in the country. The weather was pretty decent as compared to the south or east coast. The transition from civilian to soldier is immediate. To go to chow, you had to swing through the parallel bars yelling "Kill" at the top of your lungs. You were assigned a rifle. At that time, it was M-14 and we were trained to take it apart and reassemble blind folded. The joke was in reference to our rifle and how to address it. This is my rifle, this is my gun. This one's for fighting, and this one's for fun. It was the start of tearing down and rebuilding in the image of a combat soldier. It was interesting because some of the toughest big guys would panic and run when told to stay down crawling under barb wire and mud-soaked fields. I remember during the night live fire obstacle course we were supposed to crawl under barb wire with machine gun tracers being fired over our heads, and someone would invariably panic and start running. I guess they expected that because I don't recall ever hearing of anyone getting shot. During the time I was there, we had meningitis quarantine, so we could not have visitors or leave post during basic training. Didn't matter to me because I didn't know Monterey, Carmel, and these great places were just out of sight over the sand dunes. Later on I would come to appreciate the golf courses at Pebble Beach and Monterey. The soldier they assigned as my bunk mate was Tim. Tim didn't want to be in the Army, so he decided he was going to commit suicide by jumping off the second floor ledge outside our barracks window. I don't know if I can take credit for talking him out of it because I don't think he would have killed himself and more likely broke something and had to redo basic anyway. The running, marching, crawling, and training all got easier with time. One day we were supposed to climb in a fox hole and cover our head with a poncho. This was the drill when we were supposed to duck and cover in case of nuclear attack. At that moment, sitting in the fox hole with a piece of plastic over my head, I realized this is a bunch of crap. There is no escape from nuclear holocaust. We're all dead. This is propaganda, and the government knew it all along. That was one of the firsts in seeing through the fog of government propaganda that I would learn. It dawned on us that we were no longer individuals with a special place in the world. We were the property of the US Army. We were assigned a serial number, and if killed, our dog tags were our only identification. We were expendable and probably the closest thing to being incarcerated for however long our tour of duty was. Basic training is only eight weeks, and after that there usually is a break of a week or so before you start advanced training. In my case, I went home to Seattle for a few days where I met my parents' neighbor's sister. We went out, and being a horny soldier, you know the rest. I returned to Fort Ord to complete my training. Because I was signed up for a top-secret clearance, I was assigned to personnel school rather than infantry. I wanted language school, but you had to pass the language aptitude test, which showed a special apitude for learning languages in a short time, say six to nine months depending on the language. During advanced training, I had earned some extra leave because I was soldier of the day for some reason I can't remember. A couple buddies and I decided to take a car to San Francisco and see the town. We had heard about North Beach as being a great place because of the famous topless bars. We went to the Castro district to a seedy movie house where who knows what was on the floor. We watched girls pick up dollars with their private parts. That was a first. San Francisco and North Beach were becoming a night spot for the in crowd to go to the topless clubs. We went into the Red Balloon in North Beach, not knowing what to expect. We slid down a slide into the basement of the bar. There were windows where girls would be standing behind a counter. The one window I picked, the girl would draw a hand of cards, and depending on what you drew, would take off an item or items of clothing. I drew a royal flush, and she said that was a first. My buddies and I watched as she completely disrobed. I was in heaven. This girl was gorgeous. I learned later she was a college girl, had a daughter, and made enough in tips to pay her way through school. The girls later came out and picked customers to dance with. She picked me, and my buddies were in awe. North Beach was a classy place at that time. Men were wearing tux, and ladies were dressed up. The infamous Carol Doda was performing down the street, and Finocchio's Club was a popular place. It was a nice break from the military and a great memory.

Fort Ord Basic Training Photo – I am third row, second from right

After finishing the advanced training, we received orders where we would go next. Many were going to Vietnam. They told me my orders, said I was going behind the iron curtain. That caused a lot of excitement because we knew that would be East Germany. We figured out that the actual assignment was West Berlin. We stood out in the November mornings at Fort Dix, New Jersey, freezing our butts off waiting for calls to fly from McNair Air Base to Frankfurt, Germany. I waited ten days before my flight was called. I landed in Frankfurt Am Main, Germany with orders to wait for further instructions. It was Thanksgiving Day when I and another GI were walking around Frankfurt looking for a place to eat. We ended up at the Army PX where a turkey meal was available to GI's. I was assigned to the IG Farben building to be interrogated prior to taking a train to Berlin. The FBI interviewed me because my clearance had not been finalized yet. The FBI agent asked me a few questions about past experiences in school and off the wall questions. It was a little weird because the room was very dark and you couldn't see the face of the questioner. Anyway I passed because I was on the next train to Berlin. The duty train, as it is called, is allowed to pass through the 110-mile corridor between Helmstadt at the West German border and Berlin because of an agreement between the US and the Russians. You were not allowed to talk to the Russian or East German soldiers guarding the train and definitely not allowed to get off the train once it left Helmstadt. This was at the height of the cold war, and there was no joking about anything when traveling through the zone as we called it. The first impression while traveling through East Germany was the country was very poor. Very few motorized vehicles and ox carts rather than street cars. Once we arrived in Berlin, we were driven to our new headquarters. The 54th USASA Field Station Berlin was housed in the former Adolf Hitler Barracks. Andrews Barracks was the new name of what was Leibstandarte Adolf Hitler Barracks, or Hitler's personal body guards barracks. Located inside the compound was the Olympic swimming pool built for the 1936 Olympics. During the war years, the compound was commanded by SS General Sepp Dietrich and claimed to be made up of the finest and most Aryan of the SS elite to serve as the personal bodyguard of the fuhrer. The compound was where the Storm Toopers or Brown Shirts were assassinated in the "Night of the Long Knives" action.

Hitler Inspecting Troops Berlin Lichterfelde Barracks

After the war ended, the United States took possession of the compound as it was within the American Sector. My first land lady in Berlin, Frau Hess, told me that when walking by the barracks during the Nazi occupation if a SS soldier was on the sidewalk, civilians would have to step off the sidewalk to avoid confrontation. As newbies, as they called us, we were shown around Berlin by some of the soldiers that had been there a while. We were taken to a side street off the Ku Dam, or Kufurstendam as they called it, to see what I recall as a dreary old bar with toothless hookers hanging out, waiting for someone to buy their offerings. We saw several cabs pull up and soldiers get out and pick out a few to go for a ride. The place smelled of stale beer and nicotine. Hardly a glowing introduction to West Berlin, the showcase of western capitalism. I suspected the orientation leaders of our Berlin tour were trying to initiate us new guys. Later on I would learn what a beautiful place Berlin is. The wall was a stark reminder of the separation between East and West. You could see pock marks of machine gun bullets on buildings where they had not been resurfaced. More amazing was what had been done to remove the rubble and debris left from the war. 1967 was only two decades from the end of the war. To see what had been before was only to look over the wall. The East Germans had done nothing to rebuild, and East Berlin looked like a ghost town. It was depressing to see only border guards, towers, and the death strip where once had been main thorough fairs running through Brandenburg Gate.

East Berlin Picture of deserted street across border wall 1969

The interior of West Berlin was more like a huge park with tree lined streets and magnificent homes at least in the American Sector. Not so much in the French or British sectors.

Midway through my tour in Berlin, a friend of mine asked me to take a ride with him one evening to downtown Berlin. We drove in his VW to Kurfurstenstrasse, a main street in Berlin where prostitutes offer their services. He asked me to wait for him while he engaged with a girl, and I said I don't want to stand out here in the dark waiting. He said I'll be back in a few minutes. A half hour later I am waiting in the dark, watching prostitutes getting in and out of cars, and there was a van parked where girls could go with their customers. It occurred to me that as a single male standing next to the street that someone could assume I was selling myself as a male prostitute. A police officer patrolling the sidewalk told me to move on. I wanted to explain that I was waiting for a friend to finish his business and pick me up. George, my friend, finally showed up after half an hour. George was no longer considered a friend, and I was not happy. I thought, who would want to have sex with a girl that was sitting on the curb with no underwear.

My initial job working with the security agency was working in the S-2 office. S-2 is the intelligence office within the intelligence agency. Basically my office was supposed to keep track of the other soldiers working in the agency in Berlin. If they got in trouble off duty, I was supposed to know about it and to alert their superior officers. Across the street on Finkensteinallee was a bar called the Golden Sun. The soldiers aptly renamed it the Golden Scum. The shift workers would go over there to drink, regardless of the time of day. I heard there was a bar maid there, Monica, that did more than serve drinks. One time I had to go over and look for a soldier that didn't show up for work. The place smelled of stale beer, cigarettes, and urine. There was always a concern a soldier would go over the wall with top secret material and compromise the agency. Drinking off duty was a problem due to boredom. All of our operations were twenty-four hours. One morning a drunken soldier returned to barracks and decided to urinate into the cooling fan outside the barracks. Maybe he realized or didn't that the fan was outside the basement meeting room for NCO's. The spray of urine over the meeting didn't go over well, and the soldier was given an article 15 with reduction in rank and confined to barracks after work. There was always friction between the enlisted men and the career soldiers. The career soldiers were called treads, probably because they continued to reup or reenlist. Most of the regular soldiers were linguists and on the higher end of the IQ scale. It was kind of an upside-down hierarchy because the smart ones were at the mercy of the not so bright ones. One thing the soldiers didn't like was that the top sergeant could enter their room at any time and do a search. The barracks was a four-story former SS cadet school with ornate overhanging balustrade. One morning the top sergeant found a huge building stone dropped on his Chevy station wagon. The entire top of the vehicle was smashed in. Some of the NCO's deserved their harassment. They had a low opinion of anyone that wasn't a lifer like them.

One newly arrived sergeant just transferred from Vietnam was heard bragging, "I blew the gook's brains out." He thought he was impressing us for some reason. Some of the career sergeants would spend their entire tour of duty on the premises and never leave to explore the city. The NCO club was their entire social experience. One day I was notified that the Russians made a formal complaint that a few of our soldiers climbed their flag pole outside the Soviet embassy and stole the Russian flag. That was a problem that involved the top brass to try and resolve diplomatically. Hashish was readily available in Berlin and was beginning to become a popular substance. If found on a soldier, they would be court martialed and their security clearance withdrawn. It was just the beginning of the drug problem in the military. Vietnam soldiers on change of station were coming into Berlin with serious drug habits. Within two years, room searches were beginning to find stashes of drugs hidden in lockers. It takes a lot of work and expense to finally get a top secret/crypto clearance and very easy to lose. Using dope would definitely be a problem.

One of our intercept stations was atop Teufelsberg mountain in the Grunewald or forest of Berlin. Teufelsberg was situated high above Berlin on top of a huge rubble pile where debris from the bombing of Berlin was hauled. This created a 350-foot high mountain built over a Nazi technical college. The domed radar array was a top-secret intercept station that targeted communications between East Germans, Russians, and Embassies in West Berlin.

Site #3, Teufelsberg Intercept Station

There were other targets within government and military installations throughout East Berlin and East Germany. For example when the Russians decided to invade Czechoslovakia in August of 1968, we knew of the invasion before it started and notified the President of what was going to happen. About 500,000 Warsaw Pact troops attacked that night. Berlin was surrounded, and there was the potential that someone would make a mistake and start WWIII. We knew that if WWIII were to start, it would be in Berlin. We were constantly ready to destroy all intelligence and head to the wall to defend against a Russian assault. The problem with that scenario meant war with Russia would probably go nuclear and there was no defense. We used to joke that all the Russians had to do was put signs on the border wall, Prisoner of War Camp. One night I was called to serve as duty driver and take the duty officer of the day to inspect our intelligence gathering sites. Site #4 was next to the Berlin Wall and where a tunnel operation years before had been discovered by the East Germans. Since our intelligence operation was so close to the wall and isolated from the city, it was guarded by fences, lights, armed guards, and dogs. When we drove up to the main gate at 1:00 A.M., the lights were off and no one was at the guard gate. The officer immediately pulled out his gun and started to freak out. He said if the East Germans had taken over the site, World War III has just begun. I thought, great. Finally someone figured out that a fuse had blown, the guard was taking a leak, and the dog was sleeping.

I thought it prophetic that just a few years before when I was nine-years-old, I was reading a Look Magazine, and the featured article was about Hitler and the Nazi Regime. I remember reading about the atrocities discovered after the war and the Third Reich's grandiose plans for the 1,000-year Reich. Here I was in the middle of what once was ground zero. One of my duties was to give the Berlin Briefing to newcomers to Berlin. I was supposed to provide a security briefing that highlighted the places to avoid and to watch out for. For example, in Berlin, there is an underground subway system called the U-Bahn. All the U-Bahn stations are within the Western zone of Berlin. However, the S-Bahn system has a line that enters into East Berlin. If you got caught in East Berlin, you would be interrogated and with a top-secret crypto clearance you may not get to leave until they get what they want. At that time, there were several incidents when soldiers mistakenly were caught within the Eastern zone without permission. A friend of mine, Pete Peterson, was caught inside the zone with his printed orders. After the Russians read the orders, they knew he had access to top secret material. He had been in Ankara, Turkey at an NSA intercept station, which the Russians knew about. They wanted to know everything about where he worked and what he did. They were not playing around, and he was pretty rattled once he got back to Berlin. Berlin was called the city of 10,000 spies. There was a weird agreement between the Russians and Allies that allowed each side to enter into the others territory for the purpose of investigating military operations. However, some operations were off limits, and you could be shot if you got caught in those areas. Our side, the Americans, hired ex race car drivers with good mechanical knowledge to drive high performance Ford Fairline 500's with four-wheel drive and under body armor to drive through areas at high speeds and photograph targets of intelligence value. One soldier was shot dead by a Russian for getting too close to a restricted area. I have a sign that says "Passage of Foreign Military Missions Prohibited" in four languages that used to be on the border wall.

Border wall warning sign Military Missions Warning

I would see Mission Cars from the Soviet Sector drive by our headquarters taking pictures. In my office safe were pictures of former German Nazi's that were working in the German government. Later I would discover many of the Germans were war criminals that went to work for the CIA under a special program. There were also pictures of students at the Frei University in Berlin. Those students were labeled as Students for a Democractic Society or SDS. Rudi Dutschke was their leader, and the pictures were of him leading a group of students in an anti-Vietnam War protest. The reason the files were classified is because the FBI was operating a spy operation in a foreign country, which is a violation of law. In April of 1968, Rudi Dutschke was shot three times on the Kurfurstendamm in Berlin. He would survive but never fully recover. Did the FBI have something to do with this assassination attempt? They feared him as a charismatic leader of the Vietnam protest movement. In 1968 I was playing tennis adjacent to the Free University in Berlin. A dozen deuce and half trucks rolled in, and Berlin police all jumped out and rounded up students that were forming up to start an anti-war protest. The German police had weapons and used them to overpower the students. Within a few minutes, the protest was over.

I would learn that the law doesn't apply when it comes to intelligence operations. We operated four National Security Agency sites or intercept stations in Berlin. Site #4 was next to the border wall and was infamous because the CIA claimed to have dug a tunnel under the wall into the heart of the East German telephone cable system. The CIA published an article in Readers Digest called the Berlin Tunnel Operations in the sixties. Funny thing was the Soviets had discovered the intelligence operation before it began. They let it continue and planted false intelligence to protect their source until they had their fill of it and eventually exposed the entire operations. The CIA never caught on they were being duped until several years later when a spy revealed that the tunnel was compromised from the beginning. The CIA continued to take credit as though it were a success.

Funny thing about intelligence operations as viewed from the outside. One would think that once you have a clearance, you have the access to that level of intelligence. That is not how it works. First you have to have the clearance and also the need to know. For example, say a project is classified top secret crypto, code word, or whatever. That would be a compartmented project. So you need a top-secret crypto code word clearance. Also, you need to have a need to know about that project. You could be working right next door to someone working on a project and never know what they are doing. People think the President of the United States can know about anything he wants to know about an intelligence operation. Not necessarily if he does not have the need to know. There is a story that President Eisenhower wanted a report on what Area 51 in Nevada was up to. They said he didn't have a need to know. He threatened to send an Army battalion out to investigate, and they let one of his representatives go and make a report. At first I didn't understand why the ex-Nazi files were in my safe.

Eventually I would begin to fit pieces of the puzzle together. I will also learn that the NSA and CIA are above the law. They do not answer to any authority. They can claim sources and methods are classified any time they come under the scrutiny of any authority. Consider I am talking about methods that were utilized back in the 1960's. Since that time, ground intercept stations are no longer necessary. We have satellites that operate at a level unimaginable by cold war standards. In the 1970's, there was a congressional committee formed called the Church Committee. They investigated the CIA's role in assassinations, media control, and regime overthrow. It was discovered that the CIA had paid hundreds of journalists and heads of major media organizations to publish propaganda they wanted the American people to believe. They uncovered what they termed the Family Jewels, or abuses and excesses of the intelligence agencies. The end result was that there was nothing that could be done to make them change. The media was compromised, and based on current events, still refuse to investigate stories that the CIA wants squashed. As recently revealed by Edward Snowden, the abuse by the NSA/CIA is persistent. I recall one night in Berlin a fellow soldier told me he was just assigned a civilian clothes allowance and they were to set up an electronic intercept operation atop the Funkturm radio tower in Berlin.

Funkturm radio tower Built 1925 and 482' height

Above the restaurant high up on the tower was a communications room. They were
going to use civilian cover for the operations. This was a top-secret project and against

the law, so no one could know. A few years later, an incident happened that reminded me about using civilian cover to conduct intelligence operations. In 1983 Korean Airlines Flight 007 strayed into Soviet Airspace over Sakhalin Island, Russia. It was the most sensitive place to stray into Soviet Airspace. I believe that based on the CIA/NSA habit of using civilian cover for spy operations, the incident was a tragic miscalculation of Soviet air defense and their response. The 747-airplane design suited the needs of the electronic spy operation perfectly because of the pod above the cabin. Over 300 people died when the jetliner was shot down. There are too many coincidental factors involved to think it was an accident. More likely the operation was designed to excite the electronic intelligence response from the Soviets to analyze their capability. Coincidentally there is or was an NSA intercept station located on Shemya island at the end of the Aleutian chain, not far from Sakhalin Island, and the Russians were test launching a missile that night. There was an intelligence spy plane operating just outside Soviet airspace at the same time. The same type of intelligence operation had been used in Berlin along the Berlin corridor. Our planes would fly off course to excite Russian defenses, and intercept operators would grab the signatures of defense systems. I think that is the nature of keeping intelligence compartmented because you want to keep operations from being compromised both from the enemy and from the public. In this case, the American public are who are considered the problem. If projects are exposed, funding can be cut off. More importantly innocent civilian lives can be in jeopardy and exposure threatens careers. That file in my safe that contained pictures of ex-Nazi's working in government began to form a piece of the puzzle. After the end of WWII, the head of German Intelligence, Reinhard Gehlen, went to work for Allen Dulles, the head of the CIA. Allen Dulles was operating out of Bern, Switzerland and had formed friendships with several high-ranking ex Nazi's. Many were war criminals, and I don't mean minor crimes but crimes against humanity. In conjunction with the ex-termination camps, many were responsible for supplying the poison gas used in the killing machine. Trucks were designed for mobile extermination that were provided by these high-ranking Nazis. IG Farben, the German chemical maker and the provider of the poison gas, was in league with Allen Dulles. Allen Dulles hated the Communists and feared that the real enemy was the Soviet Union. He recruited many of these war criminals to aid him in prosecuting the cold war, even before the Nurenberg War Crimes trial was started. He helped set up the Rat Line that went through the Vatican and provided safe passage to thousands of war criminals. Many were given transport to the United States to work for American defense contractors. Their crimes against humanity were erased. As soldiers we were shown classified unedited films of the death camps when allied troops entered. Allen Dulles didn't stop with protecting German war criminals, he actually set up schools for assassins in South America, run by Nazis, that later showed up in CIA backed plots to overthrow democratically elected governments in South America. He was the author of the plot to assassinate Castro using Mafia hit men. When the Bay of Pigs fiasco failed to overthrow Castro, President Kennedy had enough of Allen Dulles and fired him. That didn't stop Dulles though. Because Kennedy wanted to stop the overthrow of foreign governments, end the war in Vietnam, and discuss nuclear disarmament with the Soviet Union, Allen Dulles wanted him dead. To think that without Allen Dulles running foreign policy, the world would have been a very different place. I think it would be helpful if people were to read "The Secret Team and "The Puzzle Palace" to get a better idea of how decisions are made in secret that only congress should decide. You may have a problem finding the "Secret Team" because the CIA bought up all available copies before they could be distributed in book stores. Colonel Prouty is rewriting it with updates, so it should be available soon. Since Allen Dulles and his cohorts are such an important part in the history of how we got to this place in time, I recommend reading *The Devil's Chessboard*.

As time goes by and I learn to become a regular soldier, living in the Barracks, eating in the mess hall, and going out exploring the city. Berlin is an unusual place as compared to a US city. Most of the city had been rebuilt, and everywhere is evidence of a once glorious past. The Tiergarten, the opera house, the kurfurstendamm, Brandenburg Gate, world class museums, and historic monuments. Of course there are reminders of the terrible ravages of war. The Kaiser Wilhelm Memorial church (add photo) sits bombed out with the shell of the steeple still standing. Lit up at night, it appears ghostly silent despite the bustling traffic on the Kudam. Kudam, or short for the Kurfurstendamm, is the main artery of the city. There are restaurants, shops, theatres, bars, and internationally recognized events, like the Berlin Film Festival. The famous Resi Bar, built in the 1920's, had phones and pneumatic tubes at each numbered table. Each table had a lighted number, and if you wanted to ask someone to dance, you could send a note through a pneumatic tube or call on the phone. There were water shows to music, and it was a very classy place to go. There was the Old Eden Bar with separate rooms. Psychedelic music, movies, and dancing were all happening at once. There were also the clubs where nude performers would dance next to your table. However, don't touch the merchandise. The bouncer was waiting to pounce. There were places that once visited would never be forgotten. One such place was Plotzensee Prison where the organizers of the plot to assassinate Hitler were tried and executed. In one room was the judge, and the next was the room with meat hooks

Kaiser Wilhelm Memorial Church

Plotzensee Execution room with meat hooks

The prisoner was hung from the meat hook by wire. Hitler had it filmed, so he could watch it. Spandau Prison was where Rudolph Hess was imprisoned after being tried as a war criminal. He was never allowed to have visitors or communicate with anyone for some reason. Hess hanged himself, supposedly, in 1987. Albert Speer, Hitler's architect, was held in Spandau prison for twenty years until he was released in 1966. Less than 10 percent of the German war criminals were ever caught and tried. Many fled to Argentina and Chile to live out their life. Some were assisted by Nazi sympathizers in the Vatican. They were provided with false papers and money by what was called the Rat Line. An Austrian Catholic Bishop, Alois Hudal, provided false passports to war criminals. Pope Pius X11 was also aware of the Rat Line. Thousands of war criminals wound up in Argentina and other South American countries after the war. Allen Dulles, the head of the CIA, played a part in protecting some of the worst war criminals who would later play a part in assassination attempts of foreign leaders and in the JFK assassination. Hundreds of millions of dollars in looted gold was sent to Argentina in advance of the Nazi retreat. The Peron government was complicit in the protection of war criminals. Some of the worst Nazis developed death squads to serve their new masters.

After three months in Berlin, I received a letter in the mail from the girl I dated during a leave after basic training. We had been writing back and forth during the past several months. I thought of her as very cute and clever with a quick wit and a charming personality. Diane wrote in her letter that she was pregnant and I was the father. I didn't quite know how to respond. My first thought was confusion. What was the right thing to do? I guess it hit me hard because I wound up in the Army hospital with something like food poisoning. They diagnosed me as having serious anxiety episode. On recovering I returned to work and told my CO that I had been notified that I may be a father. He told the company commander, who called me in to give me some advice. Major Minor was an experienced career soldier who had seen pretty much everything that can happen to soldiers. He sat me down and suggested that I go home and figure out if this was something that would be resolved by talking with Diane. He explained that if the child was mine, I would be financially responsible. He cautioned that life can be cruel. I boarded a flight for the east coast and took a combination of buses and military standby flights to Seattle. When I got home, my parents were already aware of the situation and pretty much figured out that if this was my child, we were going to be married. Diane assured me that I was the father and she loved me and so we should get married. I said ok, and we were married at a local Catholic Church where she accepted Catholicism as her faith as a requirement to be married in the church. It was confusing and exciting at the same time. Diane was almost three months pregnant when we were married. I was very happy to be married and looking forward to have her join me in Berlin within a few weeks. I returned the same way I flew to Seattle by military stand by. On arriving back in Berlin, I had a lot to do. We couldn't live in the barracks, so I set out with a friend and his German girlfriend to find an apartment. I made $120 a month on Army pay, and my housing allowance was $60. Eventually I found an upstairs shared apartment on Amphul Strasse with two German construction workers. We shared the bathroom, a hallway cooktop, and we had a small room 10' X 15". Our bed was a hide a bed, and we had a small table and one chair. This would work until the baby came but not much longer. We enjoyed each other's company, and I had bought a '59 VW for $100 her brother gave me as a wedding present. I had never owned a car, so it was fun to drive around with the sun roof open in summertime Berlin. We had mutual friends with children, so we had company, and Frau Hess, our landlady, liked to play pinochle for cigarettes. Frau Hess had quite a history and shared her stories about the battle of Berlin, which she survived by catering to the Russians. She told us that when the Russians stormed Berlin, they took houses that were still standing, and if the owners were still there, they could choose to leave or serve them. Since she had a very nice home at the time, she decided to stay and serve the Russians. She said when the Russians stormed Berlin, they raped every German female, regardless of age. Some women tried to dress as men, but they were found out anyway. It was payback for what the Germans did to the Russian women. Cigarettes were a form of currency after the war, so when we left the apartment, we had to hide cigarettes because she would steal them. Mrs. Hess was a survivor and very wise about many things. Eventually we would return to her place, but it would not be the same. When Diane was close to delivery, it was time to find another place with more room. Again I was looking for a place we could afford and provide more room. We found a single apartment in an old building with high ceilings and primitive fixtures. To get hot water, we had to build a fire in the bottom of a water tank. The heat system was a coal fired stove in the middle of the room, and the whole place smelled of onions and cabbage. Apparently the Germans cooked with onions, potatoes, and cabbage a lot, and it permeated the walls. Next door was a half bombed out building, and on the other side was a building that seemed to house people with war trauma or mental illness. Next to that building at the end of the road about fifty yards away was the Berlin wall. Only the death strip, tank traps, machine gun towers, barb wire, and dogs separated the East Germans from freedom. One night, about 2:00 A.M., a bright light flare woke me up, and immediately I heard the staccato of machine gun bursts. I assumed it was a border crossing incident. The next day, Armed Forces Radio broadcast that a family had driven across the death strip to the wall and the entire family was shot and left until morning. It was an unnecessary slaughter of the family as it would have been impossible for the vehicle to get past the wall. When the wall came down, the border guards that killed East German civilians were prosecuted for their actions. Their defense was they were following orders

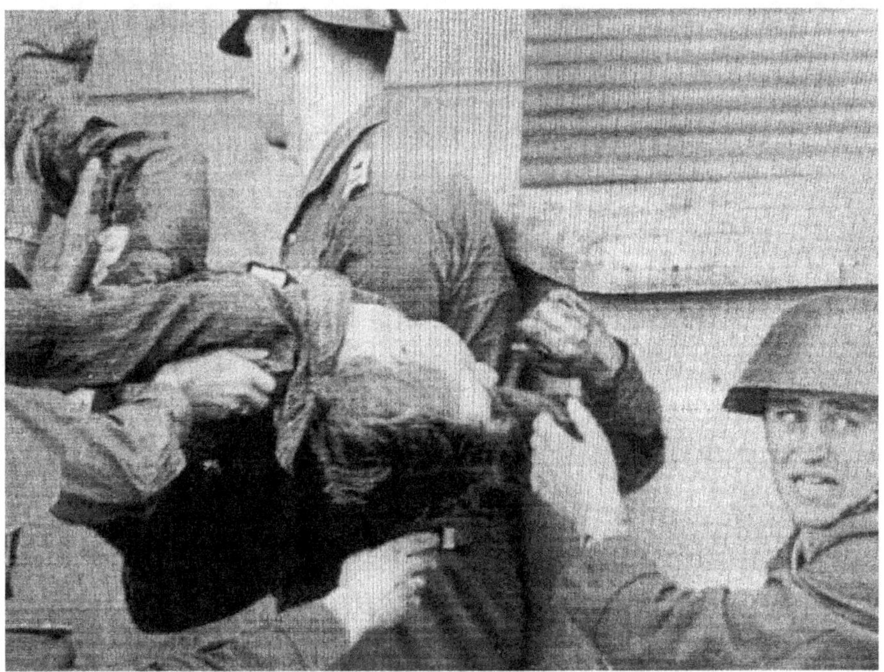

Picture of Peter Fechter shot dead attempting to cross Berlin Wall

Our apartment was a spooky place at night, and I don't remember ever seeing any neighbors in the building. I think they avoided us because we were American. It didn't occur to me then because I didn't really care if they blamed us for what happened to their country. We were the army of occupation, and from what I had heard we treated the Germans much better than the Brits or the French. We were preparing to have a baby, and that was going to happen very soon. Looking back at the situation, it was a difficult time for Diane. She didn't have a car, and taking a bus could be a real problem if you didn't know when to get off. Everything was in German and where could you go, except to the barracks. So Diane would be at the apartment all day alone with not much to do, except read. The night came when her water broke and we went to the Army hospital in Dahlem. The doctor was concerned that she was not dilating. Finally, after eighteen hours of labor, Sean was born weighing around seven and a half pounds. We went home to start raising a child, and we seemed to do ok. It was a pain to wash diapers when you had to heat the water with coal fire first, but I found it easier to take diapers to the barracks and wash them in the laundromat. It was after two months I noticed that Diane didn't want to get up and take care of the baby. Diapers were left in the toilet and dishes from the night before started to pile up. There were days when she wasn't there emotionally. One day some friends came over to visit, and we were having a good time. I drove them home because John didn't drive after our near fatal auto accident several months before when a city bus destroyed the VW we were riding in. Anyway he was paranoid about driving after that. I enjoyed driving, so I didn't mind driving them when they needed a ride somewhere. After I dropped them off, I returned home, and because it was a beautiful spring day, I was very happy to be married. I walked into the apartment and noticed Diane sitting by the window, staring outside. She looked at me and said sit down. I need to tell you something. Her face was flush, and I remember so clearly her words. After a moment, she said you are not Sean's father. I guess I was shocked because I didn't feel anything, just numb. I didn't know what to say. She told me a story that I believed or wanted to believe. It was confusing. I knew I was supposed to do something but what? She explained very tearfully that the high school football quarterback and his friends were playing football in the park by her home and she went over to watch. When they finished playing, everyone left except for the quarterback. She explained he raped her in the park hidden behind some trees. I didn't know what to believe. She seemed so sure of herself. We agreed that we should keep it a secret from everyone and never talk about it. Except it was the only thing I could think about. The next day, I went to see the JAG officer or military lawyer who interviewed me. I told him the story about what Diane had said. His exact words were, "There is no such thing as rape." That confused me more, and now I was beginning to put two and two together. Sean was nothing like my likeness. In fact whenever anyone saw Sean, they would comment that he looks like Diane but didn't see me. She saw it, too. What to do? What to do? I was already his father, and if true she was raped, who would be a better father? Are you supposed to not love or deny the good things about a person because of what someone else did? Was the JAG officer right? I didn't know what to believe. My self-esteem was starting to erode, and I was questioning my manhood. What, I wasn't man enough to be the father? What an idiot? So every time someone looked at Sean and said he doesn't look like Tom, it hit a nerve. We said he looks like my father. Yes, resentment was starting to grow. Washing diapers and cleaning up after Sean in the middle of the night and listening to a crying baby until three or four in the morning was having consequences. The first sergeant moved me back on post for a week because I was late for work and threatened to move me back into barracks for a month if I was late once more. There was a black cloud over my head constantly, and I didn't know how to shake it. Diane was staying in bed longer each day. When I came home from work, she would still be in bed, and the previous night's dishes left on the counter. Someone had to keep coal in the fire or there would be no heat, so sometimes it was cold when I got home. Berlin is not nice in the winter. One night we came home from visiting friends and there was a woman hiding behind a vehicle, and she jumped up and started yelling in German at us. She looked deranged and rather crazy. Some nights I would wake up from a nightmare where the crazy lady was in the house. Years later I would be reminded of that nightmare and what I was afraid of. We decided to move back with Mrs. Hess. I thought it would be good for Diane to have company during the day. Mrs. Hess liked having a baby in the house, and she knew right away that there was a problem. The same issues of not getting up and taking care of Sean was of concern, but it would be later that these behaviors started to make more sense. Diane was one of six children. Her mother died when she was seven. Her father raised all the children with the help of her older sister and brother. I learned later that Diane's mother had died in a mental hospital in Oregon. Apparently she had died as a result of ice water shock therapy, or that was the treatment they were using. I had been told that Diane had been absent from school for periods of time, and the school didn't have a good reason. The counselor had been concerned about her absences. I think Mrs. Hess could see my disappointment in the situation and was concerned. She told me a story about a soldier that once lived in her apartment. They had a child, and when he learned the child was not his, he killed the child. Was Mrs. Hess trying to tell me something? It bothered me that someone would let that happen. Time to move again. This time we were moving to an upscale neighborhood in the Wannsee area of Berlin. The homes were elegant with tree lined streets and park-like neighborhoods. The home was owned by a Jewish rug merchant. We had the downstairs, and the upstairs was occupied by a young German couple with a child. The owner kept a small room for himself when he returned from his travels. The rent was around $60 a month with a nice yard and beautiful gardens. There was a winter garden and a small library. One of his books in his library was Mein Kamph, signed by Adolf Hitler. I thought it was weird for a German Jew to have a book signed by Hitler in his library. Perhaps it was its collector value, although it was illegal to have Nazi souvenirs in Germany. After a year at the Wannsee location, it became apparent that being so far from American contacts and friends was a problem. We moved into military housing. Now that I was making more money, we could afford the housing and there would be other military families close by. Diane decided to work at the PX (military store) part-time, and our friend was concerned that she seemed flirtatious with one of the workers there. I didn't think it was a problem and let it go. However, when we had several GI's over to a party at our place, Diane decided to start making out with a few of the soldiers that were my coworkers and friends. It was embarrassing for everyone. When everyone was gone, I brought up the situation with Diane, wanting an explanation why she did that. She didn't seem to understand what was wrong and down played it as just having fun. My friends saw something I didn't want to accept.

Sean was almost two-years-old by now, and I started to notice some unusual behavior. After a party or having a few friends over and there was drinking with drinks left out, Sean would go and drink the drinks, and if he could find a lighter, he would suck the lighter fluid out of the lighter until it was empty. The other thing I noticed is he didn't have any fear of anything. That trait was similar to his mothers. She had no fear. She was in her own world. One time her doctor recommended a specialized treatment, which I recall was a thyroid treatment. We went to a German clinic that specialized in radiation treatment of the thyroid. Another doctor referred her to a psychiatrist in Berlin. I remember waiting outside the doctor's house while she was being interviewed.

I volunteered to go to NCO academy in Bad Toelz, Germany. This was a three-week advanced training school in the mountains of Bavaria. We learned cold weather warfare tactics, compass courses at night in heavy snow with live fire with special forces troops from 10th special forces group. It was tough training, and frost bite was a problem. The Special Forces soldiers were jumping out of airplanes in t-shirts for some reason. This was General Patton's headquarters during the war, and there was lots of history attached to the place. The entire reason for going was to earn sergeant stripes and increase my pay. When I returned home from the school, I was greeted by an order to appear before the company commander. While gone Diane had driven the car without a license and was stopped several times for speeding and breaking some traffic laws. Anyway I was to be punished since they couldn't punish her. They took away my driving privileges for a month. So now I would have to take a bus or ride a bike to work, which was about five miles away. Coincidentally there was an inspector general that had just been assigned over all of West Germany and Berlin ASA units. His name was the same exact name as mine. Someone asked if we were related as he was coming to Berlin the next week. I said probably. The next day, the driving restriction was lifted. Incidentally the captain that had restricted me had been an asshole to a lot of people apparently because he was cautioned to knock it off or he would be reassigned from his position. One time when I was assigned as a duty driver, I was supposed to pick him up at his house in the morning. I was instructed to open the door for him so his wife could see him being treated like a big shot. We all knew about which officers were prima donnas. One time a classified secret cable came in from Frankfurt. It stated that a general was visiting Berlin and would be staying at the Adlon Hotel by the Brandenburg Gate (Picture #8 – Brandenburg Gate). It specified which brandy he required and his itinerary. This was an excuse to tour Berlin and be treated like royalty. These generals didn't dare see combat. They were politicians and only cared about advancing their careers. The other pompous asses were the CIA types who would strut around like Gestapo. They didn't have a clue what we were doing because they didn't have a need to know.

Brandenburg Gate

What we later discovered about the CIA would shock the American taxpayer. I think the word arrogant would best describe the history of the CIA, along with incompetent. In January of 1968, the USS Pueblo was seized by North Korean patrol boats. The Pueblo was a spy ship doing on the water what we were doing on land. The North Koreans claimed the boat had entered within the twelve-mile zone of their waters. It was established the ship was fifteen miles or three miles outside their waters. They confiscated intelligence manuals, equipment, and codes. President Johnson didn't want to escalate tensions in the area, so didn't do anything to rescue the boat. Another earlier CIA/NSA fiasco was the Gulf of Tonkin incident that basically was the pretext to start the Vietnam War. Two intelligence ships, Turner Joy and Maddox, incorrectly reported they were being fired on. They realized they were seeing phantom radar returns from wave action and not North Vietnamese patrol craft. President Johnson used this false information to declare war on North Vietnam and started bombing.

Reinhard Gehlen – Ex Nazi Intelligence Chief

After the end of the war in Europe, the CIA made a deal with the head of Nazi intelligence. His name was Reinhard Gehlen (Picture #9 – Reinhard Gehlen). He offered his services and agents in exchange for immunity. The Gehlen organization, now part of the CIA, became the eyes and ears of western intelligence in soviet Russia. Unfortunately the agents had been compromised by soviet intelligence, and thousands of agents and civilian assets were killed. It was Kim Philby, a CIA asset, that was a Soviet double agent who identified the agents inside the Soviet Union. Some of these CIA geniuses later wound up involved with the disastrous Bay of Pigs fiasco and the

Vietnam War. It was said President Kennedy wanted to break the CIA into a thousand pieces after the Bay of Pigs debacle. Another CIA project was Project Paperclip. This program resulted in over sixteen hundred German war criminals being given cover to work in the US space program, chemical weapons, and other defense department programs. Wernher Von Braun and his team of scientists were given cover to enter the United States to work on the space program. Wernher Von Braun would be called the father of the space program. During the war, he was responsible for designing the V2 rockets that pummeled England. The forced labor camps that provided the labor for the program resulted in thousands of prisoners' deaths. The program was classified for many years after the war. The end result was that the thousands of war criminals that ran the death camps hunted down jews, homosexuals, the mentally ill, and political enemies of the state were allowed to go free. The gestapo agents went back to being lawyers and police in the new German government. A few years before, they were torturing and killing millions of human beings. When the war was over, the allies and the Soviets tried to round up as many scientists as could be found.

My files in Berlin that contained photographs and information on ex Nazis living in Berlin eventually started to make sense why they were no longer considered of interest. Allen Dulles, the soon to be CIA chief, after the war was sympathetic to the Nazi war criminals and protected many of them, even assisting them in escaping prosecution by developing the Rat Line which allowed many to travel to South America. Even the Vatican was involved with the escape route. Allen Dulles was not trusted by President Truman or President Eisenhower. When President Kennedy fired Dulles as head of the CIA, it was Kennedy's death sentence. Kennedy knew Allen Dulles was involved in the assassination of foreign leaders and overturning democratic elections to install new leaders. He was instrumental in over throwing the elected government in Iran and in Vietnam. He also oversaw the Bay of Pigs fiasco. Allen Dulles was running his own foreign policy in opposition to the elected government of the United States. Because of him, the Cold War was started even before the ink was dry on the surrender of Nazi Germany. The new enemy was the Soviet Union, and the military industrial complex was all in favor of supplying the needed armaments to fight this war. When President Truman retired, he said that he regretted ever forming the CIA as they had become a government within the government. Eisenhower didn't trust the CIA either. He warned, "Be careful of the military industrial complex."

The Germans had excelled in aircraft production with development of the first jet engine. The Me 262 jet fighter could fly in excess of 500 mph, much faster than any conventional aircraft at the time (#10 Picture of Messerschmitt ME262 Jet Fighter). The Horton brothers had developed the flying wing and even engineered a sort of radar absorbing epoxy type laminate, way ahead of anything the allies had produced.

ME 262 Jet Fighter

Horton Flying Wing

The only thing that prevented the Nazis from defeating the allies was timing and misdirection by Hitler. A fortunate miscalculation by Hitler was his reluctance to develop the atom bomb. Germany had the scientific knowledge but not the will to invest in the technology. What the Germans did almost develop was a dirty bomb that would spread radiation over large populated areas. The dirty bombs could be deployed over major European and US cities based on advances in the V2 rockets. Fortunately they didn't have the money or leadership to develop a program until too late into the war.

To earn more money, I tried out for soldier of the month, and on earning that award, received the opportunity to be a courier and have extra pay. This amounted to taking the duty train from Berlin to Frankfurt and deliver the bags of raw intelligence to the IG Farben building. The IG Farben building was where Zyklon B gas was developed by Bayer and Farben. We, the ASA, had our headquarters there as did other military units. As courier we hauled the mail bags of top-secret material in teams of two, each armed with a 45 pistol. No one ever had an incident or lost a bag. We were told that we were not supposed to talk with Russian guards that were outside the train once inside East Germany. However, we traded Playboy magazines, pistol lighters, or cigarettes for items like Russian belts, hats, insignia, or flags. If caught we could be court martialed, and article 15 was the usual punishment, but no one got caught that I was aware of. The simple reason that we were not supposed to communicate with the Russians was more than likely because we could see that the cold war was a joke. The Russian troops were under clothed, underfed, bored, and poorly paid, if at all. The Russians had been completely destroyed by the war, and they had to steal light bulbs from the Eastern zone after the war because they didn't have any or enough of the basics. Russia lost an estimated 26 million people during the war, both military and civilian. The cold war was propaganda. Our intelligence operations were aware of the dire economic situation in Russian occupied zones of the Soviet Union. As Eisenhower said, beware of the military industrial complex. The cold war was about money, and an enemy was needed to preserve that arrangement. Speaking of nukes, I recall that while in Berlin, as a single soldier, I was looking for something to do and I saw a tour of the Tempelhof tunnels. Tempelhof Airport was the second largest building in the world after the pentagon at the time

Tempelhof Airport Bldg

During the war, Hitler had a Messerschmitt factory inside the tunnels, a full field hospital, and other weapons and bunkers. When I was there in 1967, there were tunnels going down several stories under the airport. I believe there were five stories underground. When the Russians seized the airport in 1945, they flooded the tunnels and put explosives in some, according to some sources. However, I believe that we were using the tunnels to store tactical nukes. Huge bays beneath the airport were being restored, and the work was classified. The military attempted to hide from the public that the tunnels existed. No tours were allowed after that time I was there. Mysteriously you couldn't find any references to the tunnels for many years. I thought that was curious for such a large structure to try and hide its history. As far as I know, those tunnels have never been explored. The airport was closed in the current era and now used as a movie set and shelter for the homeless. The building is a reminder of the architectural design of buildings during the third Reich. Albert Speer and Herman Goering were involved in the building design.

I recall when I was picking up people at the airport, there was a photographer that took photos of arriving passengers, and I thought that curious. Looking back he probably provided pictures of arriving personnel that were later utilized by the Stazi and Russian intelligence. There wasn't much that was missed by the spies in Berlin. When the wall came down, the East German files were opened up to the public. What was discovered amazed those that were photographed, spied on, and to the embarrassment of those that were identified as working for the Stasi. Relatives turned in their own relatives for speaking their minds against the East German regime. Some family members were arrested and imprisoned because they were anti-communist. The Stasi were everywhere watching for traitors to their communist police state. The Gestapo tactics didn't stop with arrest. The accused were tortured and forced to give up others who were against the state. All of those files were preserved and now archived in West Berlin. What surprised people was how willing people were to turn in their own family members and even spouses. One man applied for a passport to travel to West Germany. He was arrested and put in jail for a year. Everyone was encouraged to spy on each other, and after the wall came down, many still suffered from stress because they couldn't trust anyone. Today it is easier to spy on each other because of the modern advances in technology.

We decided to take a vacation and drive to Rome, or as far as we could go in the time available. I believe we had a week off. We had a driver drive our VW to Helmstedt where we picked up the car at the train station. We drove all day through West Germany, Austria, Switzerland, and into Italy. We didn't have much money, and Sean was in the back seat in his car seat. We stopped in Berchtesgarden and other places like Vienna just for a meal or quick stop. We drove on up over Brenner Pass, where the VW just stopped and couldn't go until the motor cooled down. We stopped in Verona, Italy for the first night. The next day, we drove to Venice for a tour of the canals and the Murano Glass factory. We made it to Rome in two days, and because it was too late to find a hotel, we slept in the car until morning when we could find a room. I remember we somehow found a room run by the nuns outside the Vatican. It was very reasonable and walking distance to St. Peters. We went to a mass where Sean started crying and the Pope acknowledged him, which we thought was amazing. We toured the main tourist points and left Rome for our return drive back to Germany. About ten at night, the VW engine blew. Literally the engine came apart. That probably was because the green light was on the entire time we drove, and I later figured out that meant low oil. Anyway a milk truck stopped and tied a rope about ten feet long to the front of the VW and towed us under a bridge about two miles away. We had no idea where we were going because the driver only spoke Italian. I figured out he was taking us to a shop, and sure enough we were dropped off at a repair shop with a restaurant. There was a room above the shop we could stay in for the night. The next day, the mechanic told me that the engine had to be rebuilt. He said they could do it in a day or so but had to go to Balogna to get parts. We sat outside on an old car seat while they worked. I didn't have more than a few dollars cash and a check book. After the motor was rebuilt, they charged me $100. They took my check, and off we went. Only problem was the VW couldn't go more than forty-five miles per hour. That could be an issue on the autobahn. Nevertheless, we made it to Helmstedt, and after spending the night at a local hotel, caught the duty train to Berlin. The VW had to be driven to Berlin by a duty driver because the rule was that if you have a top-secret security clearance, you could not drive your own vehicle through the Eastern zone. What I didn't know was that the drive from Helmstedt to Berlin was timed. You were given a certain amount of driving time from the time you left Helmstedt. After a day or so back in Berlin, the first sergeant called me into his office to warn me that the duty driver was looking for me and he wasn't happy. He had been stopped by the East German border guards at the Berlin check point. Because he was two hours over due, he was interrogated and held for six hours in detention while they deliberated his situation. Needless to say, I was the cause of his bad experience. Had the duty driver known about the problem, he never would have agreed to drive the car. I paid him extra for his time and I was allowed to live another day. One thing that I was beginning to accept was the lack of communication between Diane and I. She would go silent for long periods and be in her own world. Going sightseeing with a two-year-old wasn't exactly the best way to travel. I became frustrated with him, and he was frustrated with me. It was a lot to ask a two-year-old child to behave under the conditions we were in. Actually it was amazing the things we were able to see and experience on our limited budget. There was another trip we took a year previously. One of my friends, Lou Saggiani, was getting married to a French girl, and they were going to have a wedding in Dijon, France. Diane and I drove by ourselves after leaving Sean with another couple. The trip was non-eventful until we got to Paris. Not knowing what traffic would be like driving in Paris, I was in for a surprise. It was crazy traffic with no rules of the road. It was a free for all, and after driving for twelve hours straight, not a good time to be hit with that stress. I stopped and asked a French traffic cop for directions to the Eiffel Tower. He smirked and said Detour Eiffel. He pointed in some direction. I didn't find it. So we drove another hour into the countryside and finding that shops and everyone seemed to go to bed early, couldn't find a place to stay. Diane didn't drive, but I couldn't keep my eyes open any longer. She wanted to drive and immediately went over the bank of the road. Somehow we were able get out of the ditch. We continued to drive until we saw a light over a building that looked like a small hotel. We were able to have a meal and go to sleep where I proceeded to throw up in the bidet. I didn't know why they had two toilets. The next morning, we went downstairs for breakfast, and after finally enjoying a meal, we were ready to proceed on our trip to Dijon. When we went outside and looked at the sign, it read the home of Victor Hugo. We proceeded down the road to Dijon until we had a blow out on one of the tires. The wheel bolts were frozen, and the tool kit didn't seem to work to loosen them. Fortunately we were close to a garage and gas station. I went to ask the station owner to assist me, and he shut the door with the comment American. I said what are you talking about? He and his German Shepherd dog would not open the door. I waited outside until he finally opened the door and came out to help. I didn't understand his reluctance until I later learned that the French were not at all happy about Nato and our presence in France. It was a complicated relationship with a history that didn't make sense to me. It could have been the French found out the CIA wanted to assassinate DeGaulle, the president of France. We drove on to Dijon, stopping at some castle ruins where I just drove up to the castle. Apparently that was not allowed because a local farmer tried to chase me away. I ignored him and took pictures of the ruins anyway. We attended the wedding, and everything was very formal with a huge dinner and more wine glasses than I had ever seen before. I think each setting had six or seven glasses. The atmosphere was a little less friendly toward us Americans, and it just seemed guarded for some reason. The Italians were much friendlier, and later I learned that there were rivalries between the French and Italians that went back centuries. There was so much history between these countries, and they were so close together. I made a comment to one of the bride's family that he reminded me of my grandfather, an Italian. He was offended. It bothered me for a long time. It was confusing because I didn't mean to be insulting, and obviously I didn't know their history. In these countries, being geographically right next door to each other, they may have fought against each other in past wars and maybe relatives were killed in battle.

The Italians fought the French. The French fought the Germans. Maybe they all fought each other at one time. I just wanted to enjoy the experience, not be the ugly American. Back in Berlin from our trips to Italy and France, we started to have more things to do that were fun. We joined a bowling league with friends, went to movies, had dinner parties, and played cards with friends. The summers in Berlin are beautiful, and like I said before, Berlin was like a big park. The zoo was one of the best in the world, and there were art classes offered to military families with other activities. I started to notice that for some reason I had a dark cloud hanging over my head, a feeling of impending doom. I started to focus on the sky as in seeing an approaching storm. There were storm clouds hanging in the distance. I was externalizing what was going on within. What I didn't know at the time was that my anger or frustration was just beneath the surface being repressed.

It was getting close to the end of my tour of duty in Berlin, and we were going to have to go back to the states for my last six months of duty. I was assigned to Ft. Devens, Mass, the home of the ASA training school. Housing was super expensive in Mass, so we decided to drive to California to see my parents and then on to Seattle where Diane would stay for the balance of my service. We had bought a new car in New Jersey, so driving across the US was a fun but exhaustive experience. We didn't have much money, so we had to drive straight through, or so I thought. After sixteen hours driving, a state patrol pulled me over and said I had been doing ninety miles per hour, which I didn't remember but was so tired, it was amazing I stayed on the road. I told him my dilemma, and he wanted to see my orders. After he confirmed I was legit and wasn't making up a story about returning from Germany and trying to get back home, he let me go with the stipulation I pull off the next ramp and get some sleep. I got off the freeway, and as soon as he was out of sight, kept going. We arrived in California three days after we started, staying in a motel one night. When we got to my parents' house in Whittier, California, I passed out for two days. We drove to Seattle after a few more days and settled Diane in with her dad, who was glad to have her home. She and Sean stayed there for what was supposed to be six months. After flying back to Ft. Devens Mass and working for three months, I heard about an early out program for GI's if enrolled as a full-time student in a college program. If enrolled you could get out three months early. I called Diane and asked her to enroll me at Highline college, which she did, and within a few weeks I was on a plane back to Seattle as a civilian. In

1970 Boeing decided to lay off thousands of workers, and as the main employer in the state, people were looking for jobs anywhere they could find them. Homes were going into foreclosure, and the billboard off the freeway to Seattle said will the last person out of Seattle turn out the lights? I was able to get my job back at Johnny's Food Center. A law was created that employers had to give you back your job if you were drafted and so I applied for work there. The personnel manager was very nice and gave me weekends at time and a half, and since I was a full-time college student, he thought that would help me with time to study. I was doing pretty well until Johnny's step-son, who was a real jerk, decided he didn't think I should be getting time and a half for weekends. He thought that since his dad owned the stores, he could make decisions about the store he managed. So shortly after working there for a few months, he fired me because I sold a customer Cornish game hens at a discount. I went to the college campus and looked up job postings on the wall. There was a listing for a sales person for Prudential Life Insurance. I interviewed, and they hired me at about $150 a month, plus commission. I was supposed to sell life insurance door to door and collect premiums on existing life policies. It was kind of fun because a lot of the salesmen liked to hang out in the office and go to lunch together. I was gung ho and wanted to succeed, so I would knock on doors and try to sell life insurance to anyone that would listen. Several of the salesmen were ex-servicemen with a few returning from Vietnam. There were also Boeing engineers, teachers, and out of work men trying to support their families. It was tough selling life insurance, and despite the commercials about a piece of the rock and the solid impression of Prudential, I became disillusioned with their sales tactics. They wanted us to finance premiums for new life sales by using dividends and cash value of existing policies to buy more life insurance. It came across as getting more without having to pay more. Eventually Prudential got in trouble with the regulators because this scheme eventually wiped out the savings of insureds policies. It was a big deal for a while, and they returned to the same practice a few years later. The sales manager had asked me to quit college for a few years to focus on life insurance sales, and after a year, I decided I had enough. My brother-in-law worked for Frito Lay driving a truck. I was hired to deliver chips and other product to stores on my route. We started at five or six in the morning and were done by 1:00 or 2:00 in the afternoon. It wasn't a bad job, just boring. When Frito Lay went on strike for thirteen weeks, I went to California to see about working there for the company. The territory I would have was in East LA. The supervisor suggested I carry a gun, which most drivers did. I decided to return back home and bussed tables at the Elks Club until the strike was over. Since we were Teamsters, the union was supposed to protect strike workers. That didn't happen because within a few weeks, all the strike organizers were fired for one reason or another. I wrote a letter to the NLRB filing a complaint about what I was seeing. The union rep came out to visit me and suggested I find another line of work, and they were willing to pay me six week's pay if I would leave. I suspected that the union reps were in cahoots with the executives at Frito Lay. Little did I know that the Teamsters honchos were mobsters. I said OK because I was already working on another plan to open a tennis club. In West Seattle, there were tennis players that played outside, and I suggested they form a club and build an indoor facility. They were interested, so I noticed that one of the buildings on my Frito Lay route was vacant and would be perfect for an indoor tennis facility. The day I walked inside the building to check it out, a real estate lady was also there. I told her a little about my idea, and she said guess what, I have someone that wants to do the same thing and even has an architectural plan drawn for the courts. She introduced me to Yusuf Khan, a world-famous squash and tennis pro. We met and briefly discussed the potential plan. Neither of us had any money, which was a problem. However, the building owner, Noel Dumas from Vancouver, BC, was a very wealthy man. The building was useless for the intended use of parking trucks and buses because the building was built on a Boeing landfill. The floors were sinking, and it was a no-load building. With three and a half acres covered and a forty-foot ceiling, it was perfect for indoor tennis. We met with Noel and his son-in-law, Peter, also a tennis player.

They listened to our idea, and after sitting quietly until they had heard our presentation with me doing most of the talking, they said, "We will finance the entire project and include a squash and racquet ball building in addition to the existing building." I thought we had gone to heaven. They were putting up all the financing without requiring members to contribute a dime. My job was to organize bringing in an office trailer and setting up a sales team. We were up and running within a week, and word of mouth was bringing people in to sign up for membership. Yusuf Khan had contacts throughout the Seattle area, and advertising did the rest. Within a few months, we had 1,000 members signed up. Contractors were hired to drill pilings for the new restaurant, lounge, and locker room area. My job was to coordinate with contractors and organize the tennis courts installation, which turned out to be somewhat of a fiasco. Yusuf didn't appreciate technology over manual labor. He wanted hundreds of boxes containing tennis surface material to be manually loaded and unloaded from pull carts rather than forklifts with pallets. There was a constant friction between us on how to hire and work with people. This wasn't Pakistan where there was a caste system. He wanted to treat workers like slave labor. He also had an explosive temper if something didn't go his way. His ego would not let anyone else manage. The owners could see the dilemma, and when they proposed making me the GM, he exploded and threatened to quit. It was him or me that had to go. It was clear he was the name draw because of his worldwide recognition as #1 or #2 in squash. His entire family was synonymous with squash. What was a dream come true was now a very painful experience. The club opened with great fanfare as the largest indoor tennis, squash, and racquet ball facility in the world and in fact was called Tennis World. It didn't last long though. Because the building was built over a landfill, the methane gas was creeping up through the pilings, and ventilation fans did not dissipate the gases. It was the beginning of the environmental movement, and people were concerned. There was something to be concerned about now that we know some of the chemicals that Boeing dumped in this landfill were hazardous. PCB's and other exotic chemicals from plane manufacturing are not to be dismissed lightly. No one even knew what was in the landfill because records were not kept in those early years. We know that many of the stealth fighter wing coatings were highly toxic, and aircraft workers were being sickened by these exotic and toxic chemicals. The aircraft manufacturers will not identify which chemicals they used because they say it is classified. Within a few years, there were enough complaints that membership dropped to the point it was unsustainable. Members wanted their lifetime membership back when the owners of the building sold it to a union for storage. An attorney contacted me about something related to the club, and I mentioned that their plan all along was to sell the building to anyone if it didn't work out. I had papers that said that in the planning stages in our meetings. I produced the copies of the meetings where it was clear that they would be willing to sell for other use. You can't sell lifetime memberships if you don't plan to be in business for a lifetime. They had to return the fees.

Now that I was out of a job and looking for work. I was referred to Mutual of Enumclaw. They wanted to interview me for a position. When I found out it had to do with life insurance, I made it clear I wasn't interested in selling life insurance. They said no, it's about underwriting. They had started a life company, and their underwriter was planning on leaving, so someone with life insurance background would be a good idea. After it was clear that I would be underwriting both life and property/casualty, I took the job. I would go to Los Angeles for a two-week life underwriting course at Transamerica. With both life and property/casualty underwriting training, it was interesting. I worked directly with the president of the company, and he liked hearing my stories about some of my experiences. The company was a great place to land after the failure of my dream job running a tennis club. It was like a family in Enumclaw. The people were the salt of the earth. A lot of former loggers and farmers worked at the company. They were honest and straight forward. Many of the employees were from pioneer families who had travelled in wagon trains navigating through the frontier to settle in the Enumclaw Plateau. This was a solid company with good values. The president, Vance Fredrickson, had worked his way up from the bottom, and that was their philosophy. When I was hired, I started in the basement file room and worked in each department to see how everyone clicked together. A lot of employees were related, so it was smart to tread lightly when you work together. All good things come to an end as the saying goes. In the case of this once small regional company, wokeism and the ravages of Covid forced the company to adopt the current practice of working from home. Now employees don't want to return to the office. Eventually, after a few years working in the home office, an opportunity came up where I was offered to work in an insurance brokerage. More money could be made selling property casualty insurance than as an underwriter, so I took the job. The agency was in Auburn where the person I replaced at Mutual of Enumclaw went to work. He thought we would make a good team. I was working hard making sales, although the owner of the agency was a little weird. He would stay late and play the organ surrounded by files. He lived with his mother and considered himself a pseudo doctor. He became stranger as time went by. The offer was made for me to buy the agency as the owner was getting older. I was in process of getting financing secured by Mutual of Enumclaw.

Just as I was set to take over, the owner called a meeting and announced, "I have sold the agency to the local competitor in Kent." I was shocked because we had a deal. Fortunately I didn't sign the non-compete agreement he had asked me to sign the week before. He was already planning to eliminate me as a threat to the new owners.

The now new owners met with me and said, "Last night we removed all of your files, and you no longer work for us and there is no severance agreement." I said it is two weeks before Christmas and that is your offer? The person making the statement had a reputation for being a complete asshole, so I was not surprised. I immediately contacted Mutual of Enumclaw and told them that the agency was sold out from under me, and they said they were not surprised because of the owner's history. They thought he had emotional problems and said if I wanted an appointment, they would give me one. That was unheard of in those days. You usually had to have a book of business or something to start with to get an agency appointment. I found a small office to rent in Federal Way and immediately decorated the office, bought a manual typewriter, a Sears two drawer filing cabinet, and a coffee pot. The phone lines were hooked up by a friend. I had saved $7,000 from a property sale. I tried to get a second loan against our home, but the bank didn't think I was credit worthy enough to grant a loan. I went into business within five days. The ironic thing about the office space was that it was the Lloyd's London Building in the Old World Square of Federal Way. It was a tourist type attraction for many years until it was torn down by a developer. The people that bought the agency that I was going to buy were not happy I opened my own agency, and they did their best to stop me. The first thing they did was contact my previous customers that I had sold to and told them I had been offered a responsible position but had disappeared for some reason, as though I was an alcoholic or something. I had secured a second appointment with Safeco Insurance Company. After three months, I had several quotes in process, and Safeco contacted me to let me know they would be terminating my contract for lack of production. I protested because that didn't make sense. The marketing rep that was leaving the company in a few weeks told me the real reason was the company that bought the agency I was going to buy told them to cancel me because I was operating in their sales territory and they were one of Safeco's largest producers. It didn't surprise me. I was struggling to find new customers. By coincidence one of the prospects I was trying to sell to was insured by the firm that had just let me go. When they found out I was competing with them, they told the prospect I "couldn't be trusted and used misinformation to get quotes." The prospective customer was upset that I was being defamed and let me know they would sign a deposition stating what had been said about me. I hired a lawyer with what little funds I had left, filed a defamation suit. When the process server went to this individual's house to serve him, he threatened to shoot her. That didn't go over very well. They finally agreed to cease and desist and never say another word about me. Insurance is a tough business, and if you are going to start from scratch, it would be recommended to have a nice reserve of cash to fall back on. I could not afford to hire a secretary, so my wife volunteered to fill in some days to answer the phone. It didn't help that Diane's father passed away during this time, and as they were very close, the dam was about to burst.

I started to notice more of the disorganized things at home. Dishes were not done from the night before. Clothes were piled up, and nothing was cleaned up. One night I noticed the lights were on in the hallway, and Diane was not in bed in the middle of the night. I went out to see what was going on and noticed that the heat was on ninety degrees and Diane was not to be found. We lived in a wooded area with no street lights, and the front door was open. Sometimes Diane stayed up late sewing or knitting. It wasn't unusual for her to be making something. Something wasn't right, and my sense of alarm was increasing because of what didn't make sense about the time, the heat, and the front door. We lived next to a wooded area with no street lights. With the front door open and being that it was two in the morning, alarm bells were going off in my head. I found her outside in her nightgown and asked her what she was doing, and she said going for a walk. It's the middle of the night, and you aren't dressed to be outside. I could tell this was not normal, and my adrenalin was pumping. Diane's eyes were dilated, and she was acting very strange. By morning she was acting manic and not making sense about anything. I didn't know what to do and I think that I called my doctor for advice. He recommended I call an evaluation hotline where mental health specialists would come out to do an evaluation. A team of two individuals arrived a few hours later. A woman and a man came in the house and proceeded to interview Diane. She was very anxious and making nonsensical statements and would go from laughing to agitated with some threatening comments that the evaluation team thought was an indication of concern because there were children in the house. They told me that an involuntary treatment authorization was warranted and they would call an ambulance to come and transport her to the hospital. I asked which hospital, and they said the only one available right now is Western State Hospital. I was upset because I knew the history of Western State Hospital from growing up in Tacoma area. An ambulance drove into the driveway and behind them was a police car. The officer came up to the house, and Diane had run behind the house into the tool shed. The police officer pulled his handgun and went towards the tool shed. I said no, she isn't going to do anything, but he didn't trust my opinion. I convinced Diane to come out, and she opened the door. The officer took her to the ambulance, and I didn't want to watch them drive away. Later that day, I went to Western State Hospital to visit her. The psychiatric nurse could tell I was very nervous about being there. She said don't worry, it isn't catchy. I guess that was a little bit of humor in a very sad day. I went inside and noticed that there were many patients in various states of illness. They had medicated Diane, and she was angry, confused, not very talkative. This was a living nightmare, and it was going to get a lot worse. For someone who has not had to go through involuntary committing someone, it is not something you ever can prepare for. Committing a wife, son, or daughter is like convicting them. Your natural instinct is to protect your family. Now you are putting them in harm's way to protect them. Western State Hospital had a reputation where people were institutionalized against their will and housed with other inmates that could cause them bodily harm. You can't intervene in their treatment while they are there or know what they are going to experience. The law is clear though. After seventy-two hours of involuntary treatment, they have to be released unless a court decides they need more treatment or other options. In this case, the court appointed attorney in Seattle wanted Diane released immediately.

She was not concerned about further treatment, evaluation, or the fact that there are children in the house that are alone with her while I am at work. I wanted the court to order her to see a psychiatrist for follow up care, treatment, and someone to monitor the psychoactive drugs that would be prescribed.

I had been able to have my doctor recommend another doctor in their clinic that could see her before she was released. The attorney that was assigned to represent Diane wanted to argue with me about her treatment and thought it wasn't necessary and what kind of a husband was I? All she wanted to do was let her walk out of there without a thought about what would happen next. I was totally frustrated because she wanted to treat me like the bad guy. I did take Diane over to the doctor for her first appointment, and after an interview, he prescribed anti-psychotic drugs. They all have side effects and need to be monitored. We both met with the doctor, and he felt she could return home with instructions on how to take the medications and pretty much what to expect. He was a voice of calm and reason in a storm of emotions. I was very happy that I had insisted on having a treatment plan in place before we left for home. I think phone calls were made to the court, and Diane was released to go home. Anyone going through this process is going to feel guilty because you have to make decisions that you would never think you would have to. If you are the reason your wife or child is committed to a mental hospital, they are going to resent you, and I didn't want to have to make that decision. However, at some point, you don't have a choice. If you are confined with a person during a psychotic episode, something has to give, and if you don't get them help, that is abuse. There is no alternative, except confining them in a place they can't hurt themselves and anyone else. They need to be medicated by people that know what they are doing. In Diane's case, she was taking medication. I believe lithium, Navane, Cogentin were a few of the anti-psychotic medications used at the time. She broke through those and had episodes anyway. In her case, they confined her in a padded room and used shock therapy to bring her out of the episode. One time I visited her at the psychiatric facility.

A male patient came up to me and said, "Your wife gives me hand jobs for cigarettes." I went to the psychiatric nurse in charge and complained about what was said.

She said, "We can't watch them every minute." Diane was still mentally ill once released. Each year, about Easter, she would have a recurrence. Fortunately there were alternatives to Western State Hospital. Fairfax Psychiatric Hospital in Kirkland, Washington is a modern facility with a well-staffed treatment team. When visiting the hospital, I noticed many young patients and I asked the doctor why so many? He said some of the drugs that were taken were causing permanent damage and they didn't know what was in the drugs. After one such episode, the dam broke and she revealed some of the buried experiences from her past. I had learned that her mother had died in a mental hospital in Oregon when she was seven. When her dad passed away, that seemed to set off the avalanche of emotions that she had kept at bay over the years. Diane liked to knit and sew. One day she had sewn a green sixty-nine on her white dress. I noticed the sixty-nine and that it was green. Her maiden name was Green. She revealed that when she was young, probably five or six, her uncle that lived with them had forced her to perform oral sex on him. In her mind, she thought her mother had found out and this was the reason she had died. It also came out that the father of Sean was not a rapist but a frequent sex partner that used to visit her at night by climbing through her window. The contractor that had built the house we bought had sex with her while we were building it. A lot of things started to make sense that were confusing. The sort of promiscuous behavior at parties with other men around and inappropriate suggestions to children about sexual practices. I remember my daughter having a boyfriend over and Diane suggesting they have sex and flirting with the boys. My daughter was four-teen-years-old. Diane said she started having sex at fourteen, so no big deal. For someone to think that children can be sexually abused and not suffer or be stimulated in unpredictable ways is ridiculous. Something has to give, and as they say, once traumatized, always traumatized. My own way of thinking was beginning to be more tolerant of abnormal behavior. Reality can be defined in many ways, and once I started to question my own reality, it was time to get help. That was when I started to go to therapy. Fortunately I was lucky and was guided to a psychiatrist. There is a difference between a psychologist, psychiatrist, or therapist that is not a psychiatrist with an MD designation. I think of it as the same difference between a chiropractor and a physician. Some chiropractors like to call themselves doctors. They are not doctors based on schooling required to be a medical doctor. I think it is the same as for mental health professionals. Many psychotherapists are not doctors of medicine. They can't prescribe medication. I am sure there are some good therapists but also many who are not qualified to treat anyone. Many psychiatrists that become psychoanalysts have been through psychotherapy themselves, and that is an important distinction. If you were going on an African safari, you would want a guide. Only an idiot would wander into the jungle aimlessly and expect to have a good experience. The same is true for understanding the subconscious mind. We are of two minds actually, the conscious and subconscious. In the talking therapy, the patient eventually gets to what is on their mind, despite resistance. A trained guide needs to help direct that voyage into the unknown. It can be an entertaining and rewarding experience and one that will reveal the unbelievable ability of our mind to function under conflicting emotions. Whether we realize it or not, our brain is running both motors at the same time, processing in-formation and emotions that rival any super computer. I guess I was fortunate to be prepared to deal with what didn't make sense and learn to look for the meaning of something beyond what was visible. Living with a psychotic is probably as close to hell as I would ever experience. Screaming tirades and insults with unpredictable acting out is a roller coaster of emotions. One minute you think it is over, and it starts all over again. There is no way to predict what happens next. A thought can set off a crazy action. It is important to remind oneself when all is calm, they are still mentally ill.

Diane's friends would take her shopping and not realize she was spending money she didn't have. She would just write checks. She would show up dressed inappropriately with weird outfits. The worst part is the guilt. For some reason we feel responsible when a family member, wife, child has emotional problems, as though it were our fault somehow. In reality there is nothing you can do, except get them help, and sometimes that feels wrong, too. All the things that are said during the breakdown should be tempered because they are sick. However, it takes its toll anyway. They may not mean what they say, but when you are screamed at, your psyche is penetrated, and some of it sticks. The relationship is going to suffer when your wife is no longer the person you thought she was. I would think that most marriages would end in divorce when the spouse is mentally ill. It is worse than death because the relationship is dead, but they are not. If children are in their formative stages of development, they can see the coping mechanisms evolve and hopefully they do not learn from them. My experience is that both children let go of their situational ethics and flirted with schizophrenic thinking. The son did start living an alternate reality. By that I mean he believed his own fantasy. He would con someone and believe the con. For example he told his future wife's parents that he went to a prestigious art school in Seattle. He did, except he drove into the parking lot to pick someone up. An engineering firm hired him as a draftsman, and after a week, discovered he didn't know the first thing about drafting. It went on and on. Finally he was arrested by a swat team that flew into the neighborhood he was living in and arrested him for selling guns and drugs online. He went to prison, but they eventually moved him into a halfway house because of his disability from MS. He was very entertaining when he talked about his exploits and he believed his stories. Except they were not real. Was this related to his mother's risk factor for mental illness? It probably is related, even though many do not want to make the connection. My opinion is that mental illness is both hereditary and environmental. By that I mean some factors can set it off. When Diane's father died, it opened the flood gate of emotions. Now that her father was gone, she didn't need to hide the fact that his brother had molested her as a child. She filed for divorce after a few years of therapy and continued to self-medicate with alcohol. When she moved to a small town away from her family, her boyfriend that had fathered Sean moved in, and they drank themselves into poverty. Diane passed away due to complications from heart and kidney disease.

During the time I was dealing with mental health care for my wife, my uncle had been dealing with his daughter who was going through emotional problems. She had gone off with some friends after high school and wound up in a sort of commune in California. When she returned home, she was struggling with coping. Apparently drugs were involved, and her personality had changed. She became psychotic and had to be institutionalized. They took her to Western State Hospital. While there a violent patient escaped from his ward and killed my cousin. My uncle didn't know what to do. The family was devastated when they found out that because of under staffing and lack of controls, these types of incidents were happening more often at Western State Hospital. My uncle filed a wrongful death claim against the state. The court declared she didn't have a life value beyond $25,000, and that is what the court awarded. This is the same hospital that the famed actress Francis Farmer was confined to. The staffing issues and abuse were rampant even then. Staff would let soldiers from nearby Fort Lewis in to sexually molest vulnerable patients. My uncle was reminded of the incident where as a police officer, he climbed to the top of the 11th Street bridge in Tacoma to rescue a suicidal patient that had escaped from Western State Hospital in the 1950's. He returned the patient to the hospital. That patient told my uncle that they used soap in socks to beat him. How many patients were buried in their little cemetery with no autopsy to verify the cause of death? Recently the hospital lost a federal grant of fifty million dollars because of failing to meet state certification requirements. The governor didn't think it important enough to require compliance. It continues to be one of the most dangerous places to work in the entire state. Western State Psychiatric Hospital is the largest hospital in the state with 800 beds. Going back to Sumerian times thousands of years ago, the priority of government was to take care of the sick and needy and protect the weak from the strong. As of the end of the 2021 fiscal year, the state of Washington has a two-billion-dollar surplus. Anyone with a business background would invest a small portion of the surplus to save the fifty million the state lost, plus the human factor in lost lives and injuries to employees. Twenty percent of adults will experience mental illness. Ten percent of the population will experience serious mental illness. Those statistics show that we need government to address this crisis as far more important than global warming.

With hindsight it is probably true that there are some things you should walk away from if guilt is what the excuse is for staying. It could have been a real source of stress to live with someone that feels guilty for letting you down. With Sean's birth history behind us, it really never disappeared. Whenever he would get in trouble and be punished, it was as though I was taking it out on him, and it did sometimes feel that way and I am sure Diane was feeling some of that. Maybe I over compensated at times to assuage the feelings of guilt in my resentment toward him. There were certainly lots of opportunities to be angry because of his disregard for any rules. No matter what was attempted, it turned into trouble. Other people that became involved in the discipline process became angry and frustrated because they didn't see the underlying disconnect with reality that was going on. I began to see the problems as an illness rather than a deliberate sabotage of involvement or investment. After a series of incidents with the police and incarceration in the King County jail, the lawyer told me it is time to let go. He has to learn that you are not going to rescue him from his behavior. It was difficult, but eventually I let go with the idea he would sense the responsibility was now his for whatever happens. It didn't really work out that great because he eventually wound up in jail. I did feel bad because he was like a deer in the headlights. He didn't really understand what was happening. So I think I came to the conclusion that weighing all the pros and cons of staying married after I found out about his biological father and the situation, maybe divorce would have been the better option. It was very confusing because there was a definite feeling of responsibility because of the illness. If your wife has cancer, you don't leave them because they are ill. With mental illness, it is an illness first. The problem for the person involved is that the resentment and repressed anger can cause depression. They say depression is anger/frustration repressed. If I were to advise a young person in the same situation, I would say here are some of the consequences of sticking this out. I could tell myself that this is the right thing to do and at the same time know it was going to be a problem. Damned if you do and damned if you don't. I did learn that mental illness can affect anyone at any time, and if true that 10 percent of the population will need treatment for a mental illness during their lifetime, more needs to be done in addressing this issue. My journey was assisted by having access to mental health professionals. Learning about the treatment options left me wondering why more isn't being done to make sure access to mental health care isn't given more importance. For example the Menninger Foundation, a pioneer in mental health care is recognized as a world leader in mental health treatment and education. Departments of social and health services should be basing state programs based on the Menninger's standard of care. If I were governor, I would visit the state institutions that provide care and make sure they were at the top of the list for budgeting. There is no excuse for outdated dilapidated state hospitals that care for the mentally ill. This is the modern age, and we can't afford to shuttle the ill through the prison system or homeless camps because there are no facilities able to deal with the problem. The police are not trained to deal with mentally ill people. There needs to be recognition that there are distinct classes of mentally ill people. The mentally ill that are violent need to be incarcerated, monitored, and separated from non-violent mentally ill. The mentally ill that are non-violent more often become victims and need to be protected from themselves until treated successfully. We can't afford to let the mentally ill live in tent cities or doorways of businesses. Seattle is a prime example when the system breaks down. In the 1950's, state mental hospitals were closed. The mentally ill were to be treated in out-patient clinics when deinstitutionalization happened. It never happened because funding wasn't provided. It is said the King County jail is now a warehouse for the mentally ill. As a consequence of living with a person that was mentally ill reminded me of Kipling's poem "If"; "If you can keep your head when all about you are losing theirs and blaming it on you." That line came to me often, and once having gone through that experience, my tolerance for crazy was gone. No longer could I rationalize what didn't make sense as had been the case previously. I think in my case, my tolerance level for crazy became so clouded that at times my thinking was unbalanced. After regaining my balance and looking back at what had been acceptable, it was clear that to maintain some semblance of normalcy, I had stretched the limits of reality. Now if someone acts crazy, I am done. I remember the time that I accepted that my wife was mentally ill. It hit me like a sledge hammer. I wanted to believe that my perception of reality was the problem. I was doing all kinds of mental gymnastics to rationalize what didn't make sense. The daily confusion about why the house was in disarray. The clothes piled up on the bed and every surface. The dirty dishes left over from the night before. Staying up late playing Pacman or some computer TV game or sleeping when everyone was trying to do their routine of going to school or work. Acting out with children by suggesting silly things that were inappropriate coming from an adult. Disordered thinking about common sense issues. The problem with the behavior was that in some cases it wasn't crazy, just non sensical, and others went along with it rather than question it. For example her suggesting to a friend they go shopping when there wasn't any money in the checking account. Over time and gradual conditioning, it became almost normal or acceptable to tolerate disordered thinking.

One problem I noticed was that when she consulted the nuns at the church about her ideas, they accepted them as ok.

It occurred to me that maybe the nuns were living in an alternate reality as well. It was difficult to stay the course under these cross checks with reality. Religion in itself can be an escape from reality as I began to discover. It may work to help in some cases but not when there is a serious break with reality. By serious I mean psychotic break. When the filters no longer work and the regular forms of communication become garbled, it is time for intervention. There were times that she heard specific messages on the radio that were meant for her. Her code or language code book was a cypher system she created to communicate her thoughts. The messages were from the airwaves that she deciphered telepathically. It was actually quite brilliant, except that it was total nonsense. Once this started, there was no stopping. The manic phase had begun, and it would evolve into screaming hysterical outbursts with prolonged shouting about whatever got into her thought processes. It was time to institutionalize her in a place where shock therapy and heavy doses of medication could stabilize her. After these periods of intense psychotic breaks, it would take weeks to return to the calmer state. I became an observer of illness, an illness that never went away just latent. The rage revealed was a glimpse into the hell that was internal. Perhaps the sexual molestation that she had experienced at age seven was the underlying memory being expunged or maybe just the illness. I found the only refuge was to be firm in my own reality and not buy into the false notion that somehow I was a contributing factor. Being passive in appearance rather than a threat seemed to be the best course of action. Knowing when it was time to intervene and get help was important. At some point she knew that she needed to be hospitalized, even though she resisted. It seemed like she wanted to blame someone for her condition, and when that wore itself out, she gave in. I was always in communication with her doctor, letting him know what was happening, and he always agreed about the next step of hospitalization when the meds didn't work. They understood what I was going through and sympathized with me because there were children to think about, too. Unlike them I could not leave and go home. I was living in a mental hospital. There is no hell. It is right here on earth.

After divorce it was a reality check. Everything that was important now changed overnight. My dog had to stay at the house, and she went into shock. Sean saw an opportunity to take advantage, and all the money I provided for support he stole. Cheri, my daughter, went back and forth between us depending on where she had the most freedom. I didn't like apartment living because one of my hobbies was working in the yard. I did meet a nice lady from South Carolina on temporary duty in the area. That experience helped to get me out of my depression and start to see the light at the end of the tunnel. Each day or two there was a crisis at the house where one or both of the children would get into a fight with their mother. Several times the police were called to intervene. Despite requests for me to return, I stayed away. At this point, my dad was aware of what had gone on during the first eighteen years of marriage and he advised I would be crazy to go back. Eventually the house was sold, and Diane took the proceeds to Aberdeen and bought a house. My daughter moved there as well, I think out of concern for her mother. I decided it was time to move on and buy a house with a yard. Because my credit was ruined, it was almost impossible to get financing, so I leased with an option to buy. My business was starting to prosper, and I could afford to hire permanent employees. Now that I was starting over, the world looked different. Living alone was a bit of a challenge. Weekends were very lonely. I had moved to an island without much social activity, and fortunately the real estate lady and my South Carolina girlfriend provided company. I decided to buy a boat because if you live on an island, you should have a boat. My daughter would come to visit, and we would take the boat to dig clams. When I started dating another lady that lived off island, we went on a boating trip with my daughter and her son. The day we picked was one of those when the wind was blowing at twenty-five miles per hour and waves were breaking over the front of the boat. We made it safely but definitely needed a bigger boat for those types of waters. My insurance agency was starting to grow, and there was a little more income to start enjoying the good things. I wanted to take my grandmother back to Italy where she had not visited since coming to America in 1920's. She had not seen her family for sixty years, and when we got to Rome, we rented a car and drove to Cosenza where her family was living. My girlfriend at the time was with us, as was my aunt that looked after Nana. I left my aunt and Nana in Cosenza and drove to Sicily where my grandfather lived before he moved to America. I looked up my family in Alcamo, Sicily based on their name only. I drove to their shop, and over their shop was their family home. They took us to see Greek ruins, tourist places, and a private dinner. We stayed in their oceanside villa, which was their summer home. Sicily was very interesting with more Greek ruins than in Greece. I didn't like Palermo because the traffic was crazy and the drivers very aggressive. Taormina, Sicily is the most beautiful place on earth in my opinion. Beautiful white sand beaches, hanging bougainvillea gardens, restaurants, shops, outdoor Greek theatre overlooking the blue Ionian Sea. You could see the fires of Mt. Aetna in the distance. A very dramatic place is Sicily. You almost sense that time has stopped. For example, when we visited the town that my grandfather grew up in, the locals were hanging out on the periphery of town. They watched in silence as we drove in with a nod that they knew who we were and why we were there. San Cipirello, Sicily was next door to Corleone, the home of the mafia in the *Godfather* movie and in reality. I recently learned that the head of the Mafia in Sicily was just arrested there after being on the run for thirty years. The temple of Aphrodite and other Greek ruins are close by. There was a street named after my grandfather, and one of the village ladies remembered him as a young boy. We ended our travels to Sicily by going through Messina to board the ferry to the mainland. Messina had not fully recovered from a massive earthquake in 1909. Back in Cosenza, we picked up my grandmother and aunt and drove back to Rome. We went to the Vatican, and my grandmother was able to join in a Polish delegation to have an audience with the Pope. My aunt accompanied her in the audience and she said the Pope spoke with her in Italian and held her hand. I discovered that the Swiss guards are not messing around with their Pikes/lances. I went up to greet my aunt because she was having trouble with the steep steps. The guards pointed their Pike at my chest and said come no further. I was moving fast to try and stop my aunt from falling, and they must have thought I was rushing the entrance into the area of the Pope. Anyway their uniforms were colorful, but the Pikes are for real and they are trained to use them. Actually the Swiss Pikemen were known for their prowess in battle against overwhelming odds. They were hired as mercenaries by royalty to defend their kingdoms. On the way back to Rome, we visited Pompei, Sorrento, Positano, Capri, and Amalfi. So much history and beauty. Made me wonder why my relatives left Italy and Sicily to come to America. Little did I know about the early history of the region. Opportunity and wealth was said to be had in America. The mafia came to power as a mutual protection society. Sicily had been invaded by every major country in the region, and clans began to form to administer justice. The people couldn't trust the government to be fair. The Catholic church used the mafia to enforce their rule over tenant farmers and their vast land holdings in Sicily. The region known as Calabria was described as "the land that time forgot" and a book by that name describes the people and history of that area of Italy.

Returning to the United States after visiting a foreign country is always a relief. It doesn't matter where we go, it is always good to be back home. At least it was that way in the early 1990's. I don't know about today with crime and political divisions. Although there is crime and political divisions in most of the world.

My business was on solid ground, and employees were starting to carry the load. I was fortunate that some of my earlier customers from the agency I worked at before stayed with me. One business owner, Bea Schuerhoff, owned a manufacturing company that she founded and built into a multi-million-dollar company. Her company manufactured Kenworth cab liners for semi-trucks. She was a small, very attractive lady trying to succeed in a male dominated industry. She trusted me and saw I was struggling to survive in a tough business. Years later she sold the company to a group of MBAs that thought they knew how to run her company better than she did. Within two years, they lost their customer base through sheer arrogance. Technology was now part of the business, and keeping up required new thinking. I was fortunate to have loyal and hard-working employees at my side. When I started my insurance business, it was just me and an occasional part-time assistant. Anyone thinking about starting a business has to understand that it is like sailing out into the ocean, and once at sea, you are going to have to deal with storms. If you think that your friends and relatives are going to support you, think again. Some people wish you well and are willing to see you succeed, and some are not comfortable with your success. The people that helped me succeed were just everyday nice people who gave me a chance. One thing I would change if given the chance for a do over would be to pick my battles better. Most of the fights that I had with people that I thought were in my way didn't make that much difference. People come and go over a career, and the more allies, the better. Even your enemies can become friends if handled properly. I was ready to go to war over the slightest provocation. Underwriters at insurance companies have a long memory, and they talk to other underwriters and employees. Once they classify you as a pain, forget it. In fact I was an underwriter, which made it more difficult to let them think they won. The thing about starting a business is that you have to be prepared to succeed. Success is defined as being prepared for the opportunity.

Queens Chamber Picture of me standing inside Great Pyramid

Sphinx and Pyramid

Me riding camel by pyramids

On horseback at sunrise next to pyramids

A few years pass by, and now I am married to a beautiful lady with two children from her first marriage. It is a ready-made family, and all the things that were in chaos in my first marriage are now healthy. My wife is a very smart, strong woman who stands her ground. Her family are famous artists and Hollywood legends. Her grandfather, Ferdinand Earle, was one of the first in silent films production. He was a world-famous artist, and her uncle was one of the first Disney artists. My wife's first passion is horses. Her father was a well-known dog psychologist with television performances. We share the same interest in many things. For example I became enamored with Zachariah Sitchin and his writings about ancient technology, and like Erich Von Daniken was a researcher into extraterrestrials interaction with mankind. As a result of that interest, I wanted to go to Egypt and see the pyramids for myself. We booked a tour on a Nile cruise that explored the ancient sites in Egypt, including Luxor and Cairo. We crawled around the inside of the great pyramid, and I was able to go into the King's Chamber and the Queen's Chamber (photo #14 – Picture of me inside Great Pyramid entrance to Queen's Chamber). Considering that there are no hieroglyphics inside the pyramid and no evidence of tools, it is quite apparent that the Egyptians didn't build the pyramid without technological assistance that isn't available today. In fact current research indicates that the great pyramid and sphinx are more likely 12,000-years-old. It isn't remarkable enough that the pyramid appears as it does without the casing stones that once covered the entire monument. The temple complex adjacent to the great pyramid are exactly the same construction as temples in South America. There is no evidence of tools or technology that explain how these massive stones were carved, moved, and elevated into position. They have survived earthquakes and floods. Somehow the construction is so perfect that not even piece of paper can fit between the stones

There is resistance to the obvious conclusion that primitive societies did not create these monuments. Cultural identities rest on the assumption that these primitive societies somehow created these monuments. The Egyptologists and archaelogists' reputations are dependent on the party line that their interpretation of history can't be questioned. Common sense has prevailed, and more and more of the average folk believe that there have been advanced civilizations in the past. For some reason they disappeared, leaving the stone monuments as a beacon into the past. It is said that if our civilization were to end today within a thousand years, there would be no trace of our time here. Considering that the earth is several-billion-years-old, there could have been many advanced civilizations here before us.

Baalbeck Lebanon Stone Picture

Undersea exploration is now revealing lost cities that were once part of a land mass thousands of years ago. What is probably the most convincing monument that defies explanation is Baalbeck, Lebanon. There lie stones waiting to be transported that weigh 1,100 tons (Picture #18 – 1,100-ton stone). Even more incredible is the fact that several of these monumental stones have been transported over land and elevated into place to form the base of a platform. One recently unearthed stone weighs 1,242 tons and the largest carved stone on earth. Was the platform a rocket or vehicle launch pad? It appears that the reference in the Epic of Gilgamesh refers to this place as where the extraterrestrial vehicles landed and took off from. Puma Punku in Bolivia is another example of megalithic stones that were carved and machined so precisely that current technology would be hard pressed to duplicate today. Why are the pyramids in South America and Egypt so similar in construction methods and geographic alignment? How is it that the great pyramids in Egypt are virtually identical in symmetry and alignment as the stars in Orion's belt? Teotihuacan in Mexico is a representation of the Milky Way. How did the ancients know about advanced astronomy? How did the ancients know about our solar system and the number of planets when the outer planets were only discovered in the 1800's? There exists an ancient Sumerian tablet housed in the former East Berlin museum that depicts the solar system with the sun and nine planets. It is amazing that historians do not question what they can see with their own eyes. The Pergamon Museum in Berlin houses some of the artifacts found in Sumeria thousands of years old that show advanced technology and knowledge of the universe that defy explanation.

My passion growing up was the possibility of extraterrestrial life and the belief that UFO's were real and not a myth. From my early childhood, I was fascinated with the idea of aliens from somewhere in the universe being a reality. I read *Project Blue Book* when it first came out, and although it was an attempt to rationalize the sightings as natural phenomena, many of the reported sightings were never explained. During the 1980's, the Roswell story began to be talked about, and credible sources investigated the Roswell incident of 1947. It turned out that the government attempt at a cover up unraveled under examination by investigators. The persons that were there at the crash site revealed the true story and how they were threatened if they talked about what they saw. There were over 800 sightings over several months in 1947. The common denominator in all the sightings was nuclear weapons. The 509th bomber group in Roswell, New Mexico was the air force group assigned with the bombing of Hiroshima and Nagasaki. The next shoe to fall in the UFO revelation were the Eisenhower Briefing Documents and the Majestic Twelve papers. Attempts were made to cover up the authenticity of these papers, but more came out eventually that substantiated that they were true government documents. The CIA, NSA, and FBI were tasked with the cover up, and as usual they screwed it up. The problem was and is that high ranking government people wanted the truth out, and they were in conflict with those that wanted it kept above top-secret. Eventually the truth will out as the saying goes. In 2021 the ATIP videos were released, and the Pentagon decided it was time to let the cat out of the bag. Video of Alien craft were shown that defied the laws of physics. Our naval fleet in the Pacific was being shadowed by alien craft on a frequent basis and gun camera video was released by the pentagon. Gun camera video showed the UFO's out maneuvering our advanced aircraft in ways that could only be from a highly advanced society with sophisticated technology that defied the known laws of physics. So the question to the public was could this be technology from one of our earthly enemies? A ridiculous proposition considering that the reports of these advanced alien discs goes back to the 1940's and even further. If China had this technology since WWII, they surely would have revealed it. The obvious answer to the suggestion that maybe this could be earthly technology is no, impossible. Let's face the fact that what is happening with the gradual release of this information is that we are being conditioned to accept the knowledge that alien life is real. We have been visited by ET's since time began, and history is replete with examples of UFO's way before there were cameras. Painters depicted UFOs in paintings, ie "Madonna and Child". There is a written record of encounters going back thousands of years. For some reason the ET's do not want to interact on a global scale with our society. Perhaps there are good reasons for this. If they wanted to make a huge splash on the front pages of our media, they could at any time but have chosen not to. The one persistent statement that they appear to be making is that our use of nuclear weapons is forbidden. We are not to destroy this planet with nuclear weapons and resultant radiation that could destroy life for thousands of years. The two recent near misses with nuclear power plant explosions demonstrated that ET's are watching our every move, and when necessary, they showed up to assist in stopping massive explosions that could have radiated the South China Sea and Eastern Europe. All of our nuclear weapons storage areas, research facilities, and weapons systems have been shown to be vulnerable to ET control. Nuclear missiles have been taken off line without explanation when UFO's appear over storage facilities. Read Malmstrom AFB incident. This phenomena isn't just in the US. This is happening in Russia as well. The reason that this issue is relevant today is that Russia has threatened the use of tactical nukes in its war with the Ukraine. Tactical nukes were at one time considered a limited use weapon until they were battle field tested. The net result is what good does it do to win a battle and lose the war? The land is useless after being radiated. Not that our military leaders are any smarter than most of us. They did, after all, try to explode a nuclear weapon on the moon until saner minds prevailed. However, they did succeed in exploding a nuclear device over the Pacific in outer space, which caused an electromagnetic pulse which wiped out communications and electronic devices. As a result of this, they discovered that a nuclear weapon exploded in space or several weapons exploded would wipe out all electronics. The term MAD, or Mutually Assured Destruction, was coined because no one wins a nuclear war. I doubt any one with the capability to launch a nuclear weapon is ignorant of the consequences of their action and unaware of the incidence of UFO interest in nuclear weapons use. Based on the evidence from past involvement by UfOs in our nuclear weapons systems, anyone launching a nuclear weapon would find they didn't work. Earth governments are no longer in control of nuclear weapons systems, and that would be classified above top-secret. From what I have read about the earliest involvement of UFOs/alien interest in our development of nuclear weapons, we are on notice that their involvement in our civilization will remain anonymous until we can't be trusted to refrain from using nuclear weapons. The last thing governments want is to have their power taken away. The power over people and their ability to control their society is their number one priority. If the Alien presence landed on the front lawn of the White House and said, "We are here," all trust and credibility of government would be threatened. That essentially is what is happening with the UFO appearance over our nuclear fleet in the Pacific and Atlantic. We are being monitored in a way that has to be acknowledged where before these incidents were infrequent and covered up. You can't hide what thousands of service men and women are seeing. I have done the research into UFO activity at nuclear facilities. All one needs to do is research UFO activity over Los Alamos, Livermore, Sandia, Savannah River, and Hanford, to name a few incidents. However, almost every facility that houses nuclear weapons has been visited by Alien activity since 1945.

Relief from Nimrud winged deities in Sumeria

To sum it up and say I can prove that extraterrestrial life, UFOs, and Alien interaction with our civilization are a fact, here are my reasons: Archaeological digs throughout the world prove that a civilization existed before our society that was advanced with a technology that allowed the building of huge temples that defy current building methods. There are written records from Sumerian times that describe interaction with alien beings that could fly and were able to explain the mysteries of the universe (#19 – Picture Relief from Nimrud -notice wings on deities- British Museum). Puma Punku in Bolivia, the Great Pyramids in Giza, monumental stones in Baalbek, Lebanon, and ancient sites in Iraq, India, and other parts of Asia are proof of advanced civilizations that were in contact with Alien beings called gods.

Since the new paradigm is to condition our society to the reality that Alien life, UFOs are real, we can now look back on how our government tried to cover up the phenomena by denial, threat, and disinformation. These tactics are usual fare for the CIA and FBI. Were people mysteriously killed for revealing information? Maybe, and according to some sources James Forrestal, the first secretary of defense, was pushed to his death for threatening to reveal the truth about UFOs back in 1947. Governments are capable of anything when they are above the law and the CIA, NSA, and FBI are above the law as they will admit. All they have to do is claim that sources and methods are classified. You want proof? After the Church Committee in the 1970's discovered active CIA involvement in press manipulation and assassination plots, did anyone go to jail? They continued to act as though nothing had changed.

Several months ago I was working on one of my Koi ponds to pick something out of the water. I was in a hurry, so I didn't take care to get my feet grounded on firm soil and slipped on a rock and fell onto my shoulder. I didn't think much about it, except it didn't get better but worse. Eventually I decided to see a doctor who suggested a CT scan. The scan showed tendonitis and not a rotator cuff tear. I got a cortisone shot, and all was better until I over extended when golfing and something ripped or snapped. I went back to the same doctor, and he wanted another CT scan. This time it showed a tear in the rotator cuff but of more concern was that the radiologist that reviewed the scan saw a nodule in part of my lung that showed up in the scan. It was recommended that I see a pulmonologist, who reviewed a new scan and was pretty confident it was cancerous. I opted for a biopsy that confirmed it was cancer. While I was not happy about the whole thing, it was fortunate that the fall in the Koi pond led to the second CT scan, which prompted an early intervention and resultant surgery to remove the nodule. The surgeon was confident that the surgery was successful in removing the cancer and thought a 95 percent recovery or chance of being cancer free was predicted. However, every six months a CT scan to look for recurrence of cancer is required. This will go on for two to three years and less frequently for five years. Even if the cancer is removed and no trace of any residual cancer cells, there is a 15 percent chance that the cancer will recur. The question is always did you smoke? The answer is yes but not that much. I was a closet smoker, limiting myself to a few cigarettes a day, except for my time in the Army when I smoked about a pack a day. The Army even gave us cigarettes in our c-ration packs that were distributed overseas. We thought that the c-rations were left over from WWII. The cancer diagnosis reminds one of our limited time on earth. We actually don't have a very long life, even if we make it to eighty or ninety.

Vashon Island is where we reside now. My wife and I have three dogs, a cat, and three horses. My wife rides about three times a week, and I used to ride infrequently but like to golf more than ride horses. Besides it is easy to get hurt riding, and that interferes with golf. My wife broke both her feet in a fall because the horse bolted from a deer that crossed paths with her horse mid trail. It happens and usually so fast, there is nothing you can do about it. Vashon Island is a great place to raise a family, and for that matter a very nice place to live. Very little in crime, great scenery, and close to Tacoma and Seattle via a twenty-minute ferry ride. Ferry service is not as reliable as it used to be when I moved here in 1986 but definitely better than a commute on I-5. Most people that choose to live here have stay at home types of jobs or just wealthy enough to live without working. The island is about thirteen miles by three and a half miles and is actually two islands joined together by a small isthmus of land. The island is in the center of Puget Sound. The population is pretty tolerant and very liberal relative to political bent. There is a large gay population. Conservatives are outnumbered by a vocal majority, and if someone were to display a Trump sign, it would be vandalized with minutes, and hopefully that would be the end of it with no further retaliation. We started going to Palm Springs in the early 1990's. I had bought a small condo in Rancho Mirage next to one of my customers. My wife and I would go stay in the desert, and one of our favorite restaurants to eat at was Dominick's. Frank Sinatra and Lucille Ball would eat there when staying in the desert. Some nights when we would go for dinner, Frank and his entourage would be holding court in the bar. Dominick Zangari said as long as Frank was alive, he would stay in business. When Frank died, he closed, and the place never really made a comeback. Our new condo is right across the street from Frank's old compound on Frank Sinatra Drive.

There was a rumor several years ago that when the hippies were in Haight Ashbury area of San Francisco, they put up a sign, "Go North to Vashon Island". Several did and roosted in the woods of Vashon, living the hippie life with beads and bangles. Some are still here, just old hippies. We have relatively few of the homeless that live in their cars, trailers, and trucks or converted RV's. The mentally ill reside in public and seem to be looked after by an unknown few caretakers. It is an eclectic place where the rich, poor, intellectual, and country folk all live in harmony. There are few black families, and those few seem to be welcomed as a tribute to our righteous tolerance of everything woke, liberal, and anti-conservative. There was a community movement to welcome refugees from Syria a few years ago, and they seem to have prospered with food trucks. The Mexican families do most of the hard work from building, gardening, and food services. The island would not have much to offer in services without the immigrant population. My opinion is that if you are going to live in Washington, this is the place to live, but don't tell anyone else. Also, Vashon has about 1,000 acres of protected forest land that is open to hikers, horseback riding, and bicycling. We have everything, except an urgent care facility. This would not be a great choice for someone that is single, unless you like living alone. I moved here when I was single after going through a divorce, and except for a lucky break with a real estate agent, didn't find any opportunity for meeting other singles. The island was written about in a book by Betty McDonald who wrote *The Egg and I* and *Onions in the Stew*. Her book, *Onions in the Stew*, was written on Vashon Island back in the fifties. Her home became a bed and breakfast and recently sold to a private party. The other reference in history to Vashon Island was the Maury Island Incident. This was a UFO hoax perpetrated by two guys that thought they could capitalize on the UFO craze in 1947. Harold Dahl and Fred Crisman thought they could pull off this hoax by claiming that six UFOs hovered over Harold Dahl's boat off Maury Island while he was salvaging logs. He claimed one of the UFOs was in trouble and slag dropped from the UFO onto his boat and killed their dog and injured his son. Everyone involved eventually admitted it was a hoax. However, even recently there are locals that attempted to resurrect the incident by creating a movie about it and granting some credibility to the hoax. All that the story did was promote Fred Crisman in his goal of become a tabloid author. He even showed up in the Kennedy assassination story when Jim Garrison questioned him about his supposed involvement in the story. It seems more likely that Fred Crisman was a government informant working with the CIA on disinformation programs during the early years of the cold war. He later showed up in union busting and conservative programs to combat communism in the 1950's. Wherever he showed up, there was controversy. I believe he wrote some short stories for "Soldier of Fortune" magazine and those types of magazines that promoted the idea that Hitler escaped to South America and was seen with his henchmen. It could be that Fred Crisman was acting as a disinformation specialist with regard to the UFO craze of the 1940's. There were over 800 UFO sightings during 1947 alone. The government was on the defensive because more and more people were seeing these things. The only thing Fred Crisman did was create a hoax that confused the real from the fraudulent. That appeared to be what he was good at. The Roswell incident in New Mexico and the Kenneth Arnold sighting appeared to be legitimate and became the focus of government concern that mass hysteria and panic could ensue if fears were not calmed.

Looking back to where I began my story as a young boy filled with wonder and curiosity about the world around me and what I thought was important now looks very different. There is a saying, "You find what you look for," and that is very true based on my experiences. Being curious is a good place to begin. Once I set a goal and focused, it is amazing how the mind is able to find a path to achieve progress toward that goal. Perhaps it is the ability of the subconscious mind to work unseen, along with the conscious mind, and in tandem they are a formidable force. I remember reading in the bible about faith, and if you have faith the size of a mustard seed, you could move mountains. I think the meaning in that is if the human mind, the greatest computer ever created, can devote a portion the size of a mustard seed the potential power in that could move mountains. It may take a lifetime and maybe giant machines a little at a time. All the great monuments, buildings, bridges, and dams started with an idea.

Most people are good people and want good things for themselves and those around them. However, there are those that want power and will do anything to attain it and keep it. Those people are dangerous because they justify the means regardless of the consequences. Looking back at the people that created havoc in the last seventy-five years, they all thought they were smarter than everyone else and needed to be in charge of everyone else. People like Allen Dulles, who wanted to start a war with Russia as soon as WWII ended created the cold war. The Vietnam War was a product of the military industrial complex that Eisenhower warned about. Secretary McNamara thought he was smarter than the generals and could defeat the North Vietnamese with the same accounting methods used at Ford Motor Company. Thousands of soldiers died because he thought he could win, and when it was clear that was not happening, he continued to lie about the strategy. The same CIA figures involved in the collapse of the intelligence operation in Europe after Germany was defeated were involved in the disastrous Bay of Pigs Fiasco. After their failure in Cuba, they moved on to Vietnam and started the same anti- communist domino theory of war propaganda. The end result, 58,000 American lives lost and over 2,000,000 civilian lives lost. The number of wounded, maimed, and traumatized is unknown.

All of us that served and those that were sent to Vietnam were considered expendable once the government knew that the war was lost. The facts were clear in 1965 that the Vietnamese were not able to win in South Vietnam. McNamara lied over and over to congress and the American people about the true status of the conflict. Daniel Ellsberg leaked the Pentagon Papers, which proved that the government knew that the Vietnam conflict could not be won.

Having realized that the government lies constantly to the people is a revelation to those that grew up during the forties and fifties. It wasn't until after Vietnam that people started to mistrust the government and with good reason. Once the 1975 Church Commission revealed that the press/media were infiltrated by the CIA, NSA, FBI, and IRS, the public were again reminded of their reasons to distrust their sources of information. However, after those hearings, nothing was done to stop the abuse. Investigative reporting was pretty much a thing of the past. Fast forward to present day, and news organizations are branded as mainstream media. Google, Facebook, and Twitter now provide news content. Since Musk took over Twitter, it comes to light that democrat strategists, the White House, CIA, and FBI were requesting censorship of conservative media stories that didn't favor the party line. The bottom line is that this was election interference because newsworthy stories that could have affected the outcome of an election were buried to favor one candidate over another. That is something that is only supposed to happen in a dictatorship or third world country. The problem is that the party now in power has control over the executive branch, legislative branch/the senate, and the judiciary branch of government. The most important part of this problem is that the media is biased toward the party in power. Over 90 percent of the journalists and media are democrat and no longer attempt to hide their bias. It isn't a problem unless you belong to the party not in power. I was very naïve to believe that there was an unbiased press corps. The reality is that the mainstream new organizations have been infiltrated by government agencies since at least 1947 when the CIA was established.

I want to focus on why the CIA was created in the first place. It was 1947 when Roswell, the UFO crash, and the hysteria about flying saucers all hit the news wire. There was an attempt at a cover up, and part of that involved setting up a commission to deal with the dilemma of how to prepare for more incidents if they occurred. President Truman created the Majestic Twelve Commission, and the persons tasked for this committee were selected from fields of science, the military, and government to investigate and create a plan to deal with this problem. President Truman was concerned that if the public became aware of the true situation, there could be a panic. The United States could not afford to have a complete breakdown of authority, and the commission recommended classifying the matter above top-secret, the highest classification possible. Anyone can read the Majestic Twelve Documents. They have been authenticated by several reliable sources both in and out of government. As President Truman was leaving office, President Eisenhower was coming into office, and the Eisenhower Briefing Document was created for the purpose of bringing Eisenhower up to speed on the historical background he was now in charge of. The Eisenhower Briefing Document chronicles the history of what happened at Roswell, New Mexico and the discovery of an alien craft and EBE's, or Extraterrestrial Biologic Entities.

The Majestic Twelve group investigated the debris from the crash and provided a summary of the findings with little in the way of knowledge about the power generation plant within the craft. The EBE's were autopsied, and it was confirmed that the alien craft was operated by and with a technology based on physics foreign to our understanding. The briefing paper outlines the dimensions and structure of the craft with a basic scientific understanding of the technology that could be explained as best it could. The engineers and scientists tasked with analyzing the mechanics were the best in their field at the time. I encourage anyone interested in this subject can research the documents for their own reading. Naturally there are those critics that tried to disprove the authenticity of the documents.

Fortunately there was a thorough investigation into the fact that these documents are authentic. The reason the documents exist is because there have always been those with access to the original documents that felt the public should know the truth. There is the matter of what the CIA, FBI, and NSA wanted to cover up and the methods they will go to in the accomplishment of their agenda.

There is the story about the Men in Black showing up at crash sites and threatening people if they saw something and wanted to talk about it. Apparently it worked, at least in the early years. Now, not so much as there are better means of capturing photos of alien craft. After Roswell witnesses were threatened and materials confiscated. The scare tactics worked, at least for a few decades. Stanton Friedman, a nuclear physicist, started to investigate the incident, and more witnesses turned up that confirmed that the alien disk crash happened and the Army tried to cover it up. The air force was required to investigate the Roswell Crash in the past few years and come up with answers about what really happened. The white wash attempt was a disaster because the Air Force used a balloon program to capture evidence of nuclear tests across the globe as the basis for a crashed balloon called project Mogul. The Airforce said the aliens reportedly found were crash dummies used in the test. However, the crash dummy test was another test from the 1950's totally unrelated to the Project Mogul test. Apparently they didn't think anyone would check their dates of the different tests.

Philip Corso, retired Colonel US Army, worked in the Eisenhower administration and foreign technology desk. Philip Corso also wrote, "The Day After Roswell". He was tasked with sending out alien artifacts from the Roswell crash site for reverse engineering those items that could be copied and developed for use in our society. Integrated circuit chips, fiber optics, lasers, super tenacity fibers, Kevlar, and night vision equipment were some of the areas that were targeted for development. According to physicist Bob Lazar, he was hired to work at Area 51, Site 4 fame. His assignment was investigating the propulsion systems or anti-gravity reactor.

Of course the CIA will deny all of these stories as bogus because that is what the CIA is known for. Their specialty is disinformation, denial, and any means necessary to accomplish their task of controlling the narrative. Based on my experience in the intelligence world, they believe the end justifies the means. There is no law that they are subject to because they have absolute power. They decide who lives and who dies if deemed a threat to their power. The CIA even contracts out their killings now to avoid the spotlight. Blackwater and their affiliate now carry on the tradecraft of assassinations on behalf of the CIA. Perhaps one day we will have the truth about the CIA involvement in the Kennedy assassination. We now know more of the truth about that cowardly act because of investigative journalists. CIA men Allen Dulles, Cord Meyer, Jim Angleton, and Lyndon Johnson are names associated with JFK's murder. They used the mob and hired gunmen to fulfill the contract because they hated Kennedy and his peace initiatives. Many of the witnesses and those involved in the plot were killed before their testimony in the House of Representatives Select Committee on Assassinations or (HSCA). George de Mohrenschildt, a CIA informant and handler of Lee Harvey Oswald, committed suicide the day before the he was to testify at the HSCA hearing. His death was mysterious as were many other witnesses.

It is my opinion that the only way to clean house and start over with the FBI, CIA, and NSA is to have a civilian board of inquiry open the files to the public and start with new leadership of each agency. The names of the agencies should be changed to reflect what their mission is. The leadership needs to represent what America is about. For example the CIA recruited from elite east coast schools from connected establishment families with great wealth. This was the foundation of the early CIA. They believed they knew what was best for America without regard to representative government oversight. The state department was the same in its early formation. This was the reason President Kennedy fired Allen Dulles as head of the CIA. Dulles was running foreign policy without the knowledge and approval of the president. The CIA and FBI recruited from these East Coast elite schools, and you had to be connected to be invited in. Wars are started, foreign policy is initiated by these unelected bureaucrats that the real Americans have to go and fight.

I remember being in fear of nuclear annihilation during the Cuban missile crisis of 1962. President Kennedy came on television and reported that a naval blockade of

Cuba to prevent Russian warships from providing weapons to Cuba. If the Russian Navy didn't back down, there could be war. It was thought, mistakenly, that the Russians had not yet armed the nuclear missiles inside Cuba, which threatened the United States. Cuba was only ninety miles away from the continental US. The military planners wanted Kennedy to launch a pre-emptive strike against the missile silos before they were operational. Kennedy and Khrushchev negotiated a peaceful settlement by agreeing to remove our missiles from Turkey. This was against the wishes of military leaders and the pentagon. However, it was later learned several years after the crisis that the nuclear missiles were already armed and ready to be launched by the Russians in Cuba and would have started a nuclear barrage between both countries, destroying life on our planet.

Unbeknownst to the pentagon generals, Kennedy and Khrushchev had installed direct phone lines between the White House and the Kremlin, a hot line for just this type of scenario when they could talk directly. That action confirmed that both Khrushchev and Kennedy did not trust their generals to make decisions regarding war and peace.

Reflecting back on what I learned about intelligence from personal experience as an enlisted soldier, it is now clear that most everything we are told about international relations is propaganda. News is filtered through the lens of an agenda by those in power. As proved by the investigation into CIA, FBI, and NSA during the Church Committee revelations and the United States House Select Committee on Assassinations, (HSCA) in 1976, our government is run by a cabal or a secret team that is for the most part unelected and anonymous. Several years after the HSCA finalized its report, the findings were discredited because it was found that the CIA withheld important evidence to protect itself. Just in the last few weeks of 2022, we learned that social media organizations were working with the FBI and CIA to censor news stories that reflected poorly on the intelligence agencies and the major news organizations. As exposed by the Church Committee investigations during the 1975 hearings, our major media organizations and social media organizations have been infiltrated by the CIA and FBI. They remain so to this day. As has happened before, the CIA is covering their misdeeds by controlling the narrative about their history through CIA assets embedded in the print media, film media, and social media organizations. We are no longer a democracy as long as the CIA is in control of foreign policy. One simple solution in reigning in the intelligence agencies is to cut off funding. You can't start wars or arm insurgencies without funding. It was never intended that our intelligence organizations would be permitted to operate with black budgets that funded programs not authorized by congress. It is estimated that over fifty billion dollars goes into the Black Budget of the CIA. If anyone asks for an accounting, they will be denied access. It is estimated that over one trillion dollars goes into defense budgets.

Reflecting back to where I began my journey from Hilltop, the truth is that I am pretty insignificant without much that stands out as unique. Reasonably intelligent but not a genius and average in most respects as compared to people I admire. The people I admire most at this stage of life are those that are willing to be themselves. My aunt used to say to me, "Unto thine own self be true," and it took me a while before I figured that one out. Conformity is comfortable, and thinking outside the box is work and sometimes dangerous.

Sometimes the best way to tackle a problem is the simple one. For example, when we visited Egypt and the great pyramid in Giza, it was clear that this monument was not constructed by Egyptians. The simple question is where are the tools? There are no tools anywhere in Egypt to explain the tremendous stone work that had to have been done. Copper tools do not cut granite. There is no evidence of hammers or machinery in the Cairo Museum or anywhere that should exist based on the amount of stone work that had to have been done. A curious thing to me is that there are no hieroglyphs inside the pyramid. In fact everything the Egyptians touched or created was covered in hieroglyphs, so why not inside the great pyramid? Another fact, not well considered, is that the pyramids were covered with white limestone casing stones. This was no small engineering feat as the stones had to be cut to fit the outer blocks, so that there was a perfectly smooth surface from top to bottom. The pyramid would have shone magically in the desert sun as a brilliant white monument with a gold capstone. Having crawled around the inside of the pyramid, I agree with Chris Dunn, an engineer, that the pyramid was a machine. The granite box inside the king's chamber was never found to have been a sarcophagus. It was too large to have been used as a burial device. All the casing stones were removed to build structures in Cairo. Some of the casing stones did have markings on them but not Egyptian hieroglyphs. The letters were of mysterious symbols. There are scholars that dispute the traditional belief that the pyramids were created by Egyptian pharaohs as tombs. The Sphinx was thought to be the head of a pharaoh and the body of a lion. Now some scholars believe that the head was re-carved from a damaged part of the Sphinx that originally depicted a dog or Anubis head or Jackal god. The theory that pharaohs had the pyramids built 2,500 years ago are disputed by scholars that date the pyramids to almost 12,000 years ago or shortly before the great flood.

The biggest mystery of all and the most mind boggling to accept is the fact that our civilization has been under the watch of alien visitors since our civilization began. Going back thousands of years, we see evidence of alien interaction with humankind. Both written and oral legends describe alien beings that could fly and do wonderous things. Early Sumerian texts tell us these interactions are true. Now today and in the last year, we have the Pentagon releasing video of alien vehicles operated with intelligence and technology foreign to our understanding of physics able to outmaneuver our most advanced fighter aircraft. Understanding and accepting these facts as true should be the most interesting and fascinating news of our entire life. For some reason, there is a sort of passive acceptance of this reality as though it could be true or maybe not. The media portray the subject as possible foreign technology. The reality is that our adversaries, China and Russia, have no idea where the technology came from. The media aren't curious as to why now is the Pentagon releasing these videos when the subject has been verboten and ridiculed as science fiction. Anyone in the media seriously considering the subject worth looking into was treated as silly. The fact is that once the pentagon released the tapes, the matter can no longer be ignored as fiction. The power of the intelligence agencies and secret government programs no longer are able to suppress the story as they have in the past. Main stream media were instructed to down play or make jokes about anyone discussing the subject. The stupid attempt to theorize that the UFO's or UAP (unidentified aerial phenomena) are drones or possible earthly foreign adversaries new technology is a last-ditch effort by intel agencies to squash the release of the Pentagon report and confuse the issue. The story that should be told is that these alien craft have been seen throughout history both prior to and during recorded history. The truth is that after the first and second atom bombs were dropped during World War II, the relationship changed from an unknown alien presence to a known presence of alien beings involved with our planet. Splitting the atom was a major game changer that was probably inevitable as regards our development as a society. How we chose to use that technology was another matter, and the alien presence let it be known that we are being watched and certain conditions need to be met to keep that presence secret. In looking at all the information available and thinking outside the box, my perception of what happened after Roswell in 1947 is this: Once the alien crash was discovered outside Roswell, New Mexico in 1947, the intelligence community and the Truman Administration were caught in a whirlwind of mind-boggling facts. They didn't think the public could handle knowing about alien beings without a possible breakdown in society. In fact their experts advised that a panic could ensue, causing the government to be overwhelmed. Religious institutions would suffer disenfranchisement and institutions of higher education would be threatened. There was no way to gauge the outcome of public reaction. The Brookings Report suggested that civilization might collapse if alien life were found. Once the Roswell crash debris were analyzed and it was found that the craft was from a highly advanced civilization with technology far superior to anything in existence on earth, the subject was classified above top-secret. The Majestic Twelve team of scientists, the military, experts in various fields were assembled to try and comprehend what they had and how to handle the unknown possibility of future interaction with alien beings. Were the EBE's going to take over the world? The Manhattan Project was the highest classified project ever undertaken by the United States. After Roswell the new classified project was to understand the alien presence on earth, and everything on this subject was above top-secret. The new CIA and NSA were tasked with monitoring and keeping this subject off the radar of every media organization. Anyone witnessing and reporting UFO activity was to be discredited or ridiculed. Programs were established to dispel any sense of alarm by the public until the government could get a handle on the intent of the alien presence. A new Manhattan Project began in 1947 after the Roswell crash. It was called Manhattan Project Two. The Roswell alien crash and retrieval were buried in the trash bin of misinformation, disinformation, and propaganda all orchestrated by a newly formed CIA, NSA, and willing media until a curious physicist starting looking into what really happened. Stanton Friedman, nuclear physicist, brought scientific investigation into the subject and verified the accuracy of early reports of the UFO crash outside Roswell, New Mexico in 1947. The Majestic Twelve papers that described the crash site, debris, and alien bodies were authenticated by Stanton Friedman after many years of research. Original witnesses that were involved in the clean up after the crash claimed they were threatened by government personnel to never disclose what they saw. Despite these threats, many came forward and admitted the crash was real. President Eisenhower was briefed after he took office, and a paper titled "Eisenhower Briefing Document" can be googled for viewing.

Roswell Article – Newspaper

The new congress just voted in has declared a new "Church Commission" type of investigation into the collaboration between news media and intel agencies. As in past investigations of this type, very little was done to curtail the activities exposed by the committee looking into these past unconstitutional acts. Perhaps the only way to disarm the out of control intelligence apparatus is to cut off funding. That the congress can do. As revealed in the 1975 "Church Commission Committee Hearings", the CIA, FBI, and NSA had all been involved in propaganda through media manipulation. Assassination of foreign leaders was exposed, and interference in foreign elections was exposed. The dirty

laundry of these intel agencies was exposed but never completely curtailed as now substantiated by recent revelations as exposed by Twitter files. The FBI had embedded agents within the Twitter organization. The new investigation will reveal that all intel agencies were involved in media organizations because they never stopped. Edward Snowden revealed that government run intelligence programs illegally surveilled American citizens that were innocent of any crimes. Telecommunications companies were willing accomplices. Instead of the press reporting and investigating these abuses, they cover them up by ignoring them. Perhaps the new congress should open investigations into major media organizations to include CNN, CBS, NBC, and ABC to ask in a public forum where were you when the border was overrun by illegals and drug cartels? Where were you when the FBI seized private citizens files under the CNN cameras watch? Why did you ignore the justice departments double standard when prosecuting one group as opposed to another because of political affiliation? Why did your media empires choose to look the other way when Twitter employees censored those that the justice department wanted to be censored? Why did the FBI prosecute a sitting president for made up propaganda about Russian influence and using fake dossiers to secure FISA authority to investigate citizens? Are we living in a time warp where reality is decided by those in power? How is it that George Soros funds media moguls and organizations that control the news? These are crazy times, and like Kipling said in his famous poem, *IF*, "If you can keep your head with those all about you are losing theirs and blaming it on you. If you can bear to hear the truth, you've spoken twisted by knaves to make a trap for fools."
We need to hold fast to reality and not allow those that are crazy to have power.

My thoughts and ideas are my own, but I have been influenced by those willing to take the risk of speaking their truths. I look back on those that paved the way for freedom of thought. Stanton Friedman's "Fact, Fiction and Flying Saucers" and "Top Secret Magic: Operation Majestic -12 and United States Government UFO Cover-up". Zecharia Sitchin of "Earth Chronicles" books, Timothy Good's "Above Top Secret", Colonel Fletcher Prouty and "The Secret Team", David Talbot's "The Devils Chessboard", Philip Corso's book "The Day After Roswell", and Peter Janney's story about the Kennedy murder, "Mary's Mosaic". An interesting bit of information about "The Secret Team" written by L. Fletcher Prouty and his CIA expose. It was first published in 1970s. All copies of the book disappeared upon distribution, purchased by unknown buyers. Did the CIA buy up all copies because of revelations in the book about the

CIA? The book was a resource for Oliver Stone's film "JFK". The book was republished at a later date and now available.

I believe that the likelihood of extraterrestrial life is beyond question. Astrophysicist Frank Drake developed a mathematic formula to determine the possibility of extraterrestrial life in the universe based on the numbers of estimated planets, stars, and galaxies. Our own galaxy has approximately 100 to 400 billion stars. Most of the stars have planets. About one in four planets are in the habitable zone or goldilocks zone, similar to earth in relation to our sun, which is a star. There are estimated to be over two trillion galaxies. There could be an infinite number because we can't see to the end of the universe. It doesn't take a mathematical genius to see that there are potentially billions of earth-like planets in our own galaxy. Some of those earth-like planets may be millions of years old, maybe billions. It seems reasonable to assume that it is unlikely that we are the only inhabited planet in the galaxy.

For seventy-five years the subject of UFO's has been debunked, ridiculed, and the subject of a disinformation campaign by the CIA, NSA, and FBI. The media have been part of this process through denial of stories that should have been newsworthy. For example the famous Phoenix Lights story of 1997 was observed by thousands of people. The incident was made out to be a joke, despite a huge outcry from people that saw it with their own eyes. So what is happening, and why now the change in denial from our government? The truth is that after 1945, once we developed nuclear weapons and used them, our status changed. Every nuclear weapons storage facility, every nuclear plant, nuclear powered submarines, aircraft carriers, and nuclear weapons delivery aircraft have been monitored and somehow part of an alien watch system. This is not just in the United States. Russia, China, India, Pakistan, Israel, and North Korea all have nuclear weapons. There are nuclear power plants all over the world, and there have been reports of UFO activity at these plants as well. There are so many reports of UFO incidents over our naval fleet and nuclear facilities, it is impossible to hide the facts from the public. The Pentagon is now revealing the incidents to condition the public to an increasing presence of alien contact. The fact is the government does not know what is going to happen next, and conditioning the public to this reality is the best way to avoid a panic. We are not in control of our nuclear weapons systems. Because the government has been lying for so long about UFOs, it is now caught in the difficult position of having to somehow admit the truth without revealing too much. The problem is that the majority of the public believed the government was lying all along.

In movies and books, extraterrestrials are described as short with large eyes, small mouth, and ears. They are called grey's. I believe they are androids (a robot resembling a human being). They are created for a specific purpose, which is monitoring earth. Think about it. If you were an alien being, how exciting would it be to spend all your time inside a small capsule circling earth. There appear to be no conveniences or comforts inside alien craft as reported by those that have recovered these craft. Thousands of years ago when extraterrestrials were interacting with mankind, they were described as beings like us, except they could fly around earth. The gods An, Enlil, and Enki were flesh and blood beings that had sex, ate food, and dressed immaculately. Inanna or Ishtar was the goddess of beauty, sex, and political power. The Sumerian texts or tablets described the Annunaki as alien beings with advanced knowledge about the universe. I believe that there is an entire race of alien extraterrestrials that look like us because they were involved in our creation. They created us in their image as it states in the bible. Then God said, "Let us make man in our image, after our likeness". Notice the plural not singular "us" and "our" likeness.

My closing thoughts are that we don't live very long, so enjoy what there is to enjoy. There is not a hell somewhere after this life ends. It can be right here. If true that we find what we look for, then look for the positive.

Tom Trigg

Pictures: